The Business of Streaming and Digital Media

Contents

Acknowledgements

Over the past ten years I have had the honor of working with so many talented people who have taught me more than I can possibly remember. Like all streaming media projects, they come to fruition because of a talented team of individuals, never just one person. Working with them has allowed me to love what I do and has given me the ability to wake up each day looking forward to going to work—which I know is rare.

While it is the author's name that appears on the cover of the book, who takes the credit, no book would be possible without the combined efforts of the supporting team. More people than I could ever thank have spent an insane amount of hours, late nights and long days on the road with me helping to produce hundreds if not thousands of webcasts and events over the past ten years. Without the technical help, especially from Christopher Kelly, many of them would have never been possible.

When it comes to business, whether it is about streaming and digital media or not, there have been those that have taught me basic business principles that could be applied to any business, for whom I am grateful. In particular, Alfred Goldfield, Rob Green and Marc Jaffe, thank you for the guidance and continued assistance over the years. My thanks also to Steve Mack who helped educate me on the publishing industry and to Michael Hoch for his help in making this book and its contents possible.

My appreciation to all the vendors who helped contribute case studies to the book and put me in touch with some of their clients allowing me to showcase some real-world streaming success stories, which is what this book is all about.

It is truly an honor to have worked with the Focal Press team. Extra special thanks to Joanne Tracy who helped a long time writer, but first time author, better understand the publishing business and kept me on track.

My thanks also to Kimbillie Pascali, who helped in the typing of the manuscript and more importantly realized how important writing this book was to me on a personal level and understood why I could not come out to play.

And finally, while I love working with streaming media technology I think it is important for everyone to remember that technology has its place in any business, but no communication technology will ever take the place of what can be accomplished in person with a handshake.

Dan Rayburn

Introduction

About the authors

Dan Rayburn

Dan Rayburn is recognized as the "voice for the streaming media industry" and as one of the Internet industry's foremost authorities, speakers, and writers on Streaming and Digital Media Technologies for the past ten years. As a passionate leader and spokesperson in the field of streaming and digital media, Mr. Rayburn is noted for his expertise and insight pertaining to digital media business models, strategy, industry foresight, hardware and software products, delivery methods and cutting edge technology solutions in the U.S. and abroad.

He is Executive Vice President for Streaming Media Inc., a diversified media company with a mission to serve and educate the streaming media industry and corporations adopting Internet based audio and video technology. Its website, www.StreamingMedia.com and its tradeshows Streaming Media East and West are considered the premier destinations both in person and online for professionals seeking industry news, information, articles, directories and services. StreamingMedia.com publishes the largest industry newsletter delivered to over 40,000 weekly subscribers and is the number one online destination for professionals seeking industry news, information, articles, directories and services. The site features thousands of original articles, hundreds of hours of audio/video content, breaking news, research reports, industry directory, and case studies that showcase the latest real-world streaming media implementations.

Prior to Streaming Media Inc, he founded a streaming media services division for the Globix Corporation, a publicly traded NASDAQ company, which became one of the largest global streaming media service providers. Prior to Globix, he co-founded in 1997 one of the industry's first streaming media webcasting production companies, Live On Line, successfully acquired by Digital Island for $70 million dollars. Mr. Rayburn began his career at Apple Computers as a Certified Systems Engineer where he first got involved with multimedia delivery for the web in 1995.

He has developed, consulted, and implemented streaming media solutions for prestigious companies in the enterprise, entertainment and government sectors including A&E, ABC, Apple, Atlantic Records, American Express, BMG, BP, CBS, Cisco, Elektra, Excite.com, HBO, House Of Blues, ifilm, Indy 500, Intel, ITN, Microsoft, MTV, Pepsi, Price Water-house Coopers, Qualcomm, RealNetworks, Sony Music, Twentieth Century Fox, United Nations, Viacom, VH1 and Warner Brothers among others.

Regularly consulted by the media, Mr. Rayburn has been featured in print and on-line articles that have appeared in *The New York Times*, *The Seattle Times*, *Crain's B2B Weekly*, *Broadcasting & Cable*, *Electronic Media*, Mediapost.com, Digitalwebcast.com, *POST Magazine*, *Internet Week*, Internet.com. *Radio Ink*, *Streaming Magazine*, *EContent Magazine*, Nikke Electronics, Mass High Tech and Wired.com among others. He has also appeared on many TV programs including CNN and CBS.

Mr. Rayburn travels extensively internationally as a featured industry expert and has been sought out to keynote and speak on the current and future direction of streaming media technology, trends and business cases at over a dozen events a year. A current technology advisor to many universities in the US, he has also taught Internet Broadcasting classes at New York University (NYU) and lectures at numerous academic institutions.

An established writer, Mr. Rayburn's articles on streaming media trends and technologies have been translated into four languages and are regularly published in major trade magazines and web portals around the world. His second highly anticipated book, co-authored with Steve Mack, "Hands on Guide to Webcasting" is due out in November of 2005. Mr. Rayburn also holds board positions with various technology corporations in the US and Europe and is Founder of www.StreamingMediaClasses.com

Michael Hoch

Michael Hoch is the VP of Research at RampRate, and oversees the company's primary research activities, SPY Index development and operations, and IT outsourcing analysis for RampRate clients. His mission at RampRate is to provide all clients with substantiated, field-based research and analysis for strategic and tactical business planning decisions.

Michael joined RampRate in early 2004 after more than five years as a research director and industry analyst at Aberdeen Group, an IT market research firm. At Aberdeen, Michael advised Global 2000 enterprises and the world's top technology vendors on the business value, market dynamics, competitive landscape, and go-to-market strategies of Internet technologies. His research practice, "Content Delivery and Application Distribution," covered the delivery elements of Web services, network infrastructure, data center optimization, streaming and digital media, and delivery and distribution technologies (caches, routers, load balancers, server off-load engines).

In his five years at Aberdeen, Michael published dozens of market defining reports and white papers on digital content distribution, digital media in the enterprise, and content networking. He also contributed leading articles to major trade publications, such as the 6-part "Business of Streaming" column to Streaming Media Magazine, "Delivering on Digital Data's Promise" for Finance Director Europe, and "Real Numbers for a Real Market" in The Streaming Media Industry Sourcebook 2004. In addition, Michael has been quoted widely in worldwide journals and newspapers including The Wall Street Journal, The New York Times, Boston Globe, Boston Business Journal, Streamingmedia.com, CNET.com and Network World.

Michael is co-author of a forthcoming book, The Business of Streaming and Digital Media, to be published by Focal Press in January, 2005. He was also voted one of the "Top 50 Most Influential People in Streaming" two years in a row by Streaming Magazine.

Prior to Aberdeen, Michael worked in the Executive Director's office at Harvard University's Weatherhead Center for International Affairs, as a program director raising sponsorship and organizing research symposia on such diverse topics as "Feeding China in the 21st Century" and "The Future Relevance of NATO."

Michael earned a master's degree in business administration from Northeastern University and a bachelor's degree from Boston University.

The current state of the streaming and digital media industry

As we get older, we get smarter by learning from our experiences—both good and bad. Organizations and industries thrive in the same way that people do; they improve upon what they do well and learn from their mistakes. The streaming and digital media industries are no different. They have matured as an industry by weathering many bumps in the road.

The year 2005 marks the 11-year anniversary for an industry that has changed, grown wiser, and learned from its mistakes. What used to be a "nice to have" technology only a few years ago has quickly evolved to become a technology billion-dollar companies rely on to communicate both internally and externally, on a global scale. Like any other technology, the sure sign that streaming and digital media has become mainstream is when it's no longer sold as a technology sale, but rather a business sale with concrete value and a tangible return on investment. Similar to the wireless market, which years ago had carriers selling their services based on their network, cell phone calls are now thought of as a commodity and the selling point for carriers is now the added features and value their plans provide. Streaming media is no different. Over the past year, the business value that streaming and digital media technology provides overshadows the "gee whiz" factor that used to be associated with it.

Over the past 12 months the line between digital and streaming media has blurred. This is the best thing that could have happened for the next step in the evolution of this industry. No longer are corporations looking to buy streaming media as a service, but rather a complement to other applications and delivery methods that utilize streaming media in their overall solution. Streaming media technology has now become integrated into set-top boxes, wireless devices, new applications, and content models like never before with no signs of slowing down.

Despite ongoing uncertainty and lack of confidence in Internet and IT spending, the fact is clear that a growing number of vertical industries, corporations, and consumers are utilizing and consuming more streaming media than ever before. For many, the hard part is over. Streaming media no longer needs to prove itself for what it can accomplish but rather how it can be leveraged and integrated into other technologies, internally or externally, for enterprises or for consumers. Streaming media is so common now that you don't think about the technology when you use it.

Without a doubt, we are seeing that there is still a pent-up demand for solutions that utilize more "one to many" applications and ways of repurposing content. The new year brings many exciting solutions. It is no longer about just delivering content, but delivering the content to the right user, tracking their usage, and bringing rights management into the mix. Streaming is now the foundation. The new services, technology, and applications that are going to be built to work with streaming will be the big technological advance starting now and into the future. As the industry transforms to meet these challenges, it will also be building on its many strengths. There are those out there racing to create solutions, strategies, services, and pricing models to reach the hearts and minds of decision makers in all vertical industries.

For companies who are currently using or are looking to utilize streaming or digital media in some aspect of their business, the great balancing act of focusing on who has the best, newest, or most cutting-edge technology is over. Digital media frameworks are being established to allow multiple technologies and applications to work with one another, giving companies a cheaper, more efficient, and highly interactive way of doing business.

The technology challenges never end, but they get easier with standards and a solid foundation from which to build. When Henry Ford developed the assembly line, he tapped into the powerful economic benefits that result from standardized processes and components. The basic streaming media elements such as encoding, hosting, and delivery are our components and the stage has been set for the next insurgence of applications and solutions specifically aligned to solve business problems.

2005 brings many exciting changes and additions to not only the applications utilizing streaming but also the business models and rules associated with it. There are a new and growing number of innovators and leaders who are helping to reshape the future of this business and technology for the better. The question is not where do we go from here, but how fast will we get there and how quickly can we get global adoption for the new services and solutions on the way.

Like all digital technologies, it is a rapidly changing landscape. But by concentrating on the business principles rather than the details of specific solutions that constantly evolve, you will have the business knowledge needed to be successful, no matter where the technology moves.

Who should read this book

This book is essential for anyone who must understand the business implications of digital media technologies. Beginners to digital media will gain an understanding of the basics of the underlying technology and the perspective required to build a digital media business from the ground up. Industry veterans will recognize some of the lessons presented, and will gain an understanding of a business methodology to improve their current efforts.

This book is beneficial to executives, directors, and business managers at both entertainment/media companies and enterprise corporations. Early adopters of digital media focused on a single area of their business, and often struggled to get even that one part of their business working at an optimal level. The potential of digital media is much greater. Many media applications have matured, and expertise is now available for hire at a reasonable price. Most important, we have learned from several years of bumps, bruises, and heartaches. With the media applications available, businesses can look forward to building profit-generating digital media services for external customers and cost-saving service for employees, partners, and other users.

What this book will give you

Readers of this book will get the benefit of both sides of the story and hard facts and figures to back it up. Disney and AOL Time Warner need to create profitable businesses for their media assets, but they should also consider how webcasting, managed delivery, and streaming can trim their corporate communication expenses. Ford Motor Company and Procter & Gamble should consider IP broadcasting and a distributed caching infrastructure to lower the bottom-line impact of their weekly CEO addresses and sales force training, but they should also look to see how audio and video content can help them sell more cars and diapers.

The title "media executive" is no longer just found in Hollywood studios or New York ad firms. Every company represented on the Dow Jones Industrial Average and the NASDAQ should consider how digital and streaming media can be used to their advantage in the Internet-connected world. Likewise, "enterprise managers" are far from *verboten* in media and entertainment firms: The path to profitability is not just about blockbusters and production, it also includes optimizing internal processes to speed up time to market, improve productivity, and other areas traditionally associated with business school graduates.

This book will be helpful regardless of the industry in which the reader works. For the media executive, it discusses the opportunities, challenges, advantages, and benefits of incorporating digital and streaming media into business plans concerned with making money from the media itself. For the enterprise managers, it lays out a roadmap for business units seeking to cut costs and improve profitability by incorporating digital media into corporate communications, training, and other "user-oriented" activities of internal employees, external partners, and everyone in between.

How this book is organized

Like any technology, streaming and digital media can be overwhelming as the rapid pace of technology and business advances. Taking this into consideration, this book has been organized to break out the core business elements of any digital media project. Each chapter will end with a case study of a real business situation. Some of these are consumer-focused stories, where an entertainment or media company used digital media to increase its awareness in the market, advertise products or services, or generate revenue. Other case studies are corporate, and focus on building a cost-effective service for improving overall company profitability by expense management. All of the case studies are written to illustrate the key points of the associated chapters so that you learn from the success and failure of those who have preceded you in the industry.

Hard facts and numbers

For as long as streaming and digital media has been around, more hype than reality has existed about such topics as the rate of adoption, the leading applications, and media player preferences. In 2004, the Aberdeen Group and StreamingMedia.com released the results of an extensive end-user study on streaming and digital media. The data from this report are included throughout the book, and a special Streaming And Digital Media Statistics section. Appendix A at the back of the book contains accurate measurements of:

- Adoption rates of media-based applications by personal and business users, both current and for the next 12 months
- Planned spending on streaming and outsourced applications for the next 12 months
- Usage rates by end users of streaming and digital media applications, both personal and business
- For business respondents, the percentage of company sites currently using enabled for streaming or digital media
- Media player installed base and user preference
- Frequency tables on how often and for how long respondents use media-based applications
- Comparison of supplier respondent preferences versus end-user preferences in several categories

We believe this is the first statistically valid study of the streaming and rich-media market. While the population for this study does not represent the overall market at large, it is highly representative of individuals, businesses, and suppliers who are interested in streaming and digital media.

This special section with hard facts and figures on end-user adoption gives you the data and real story of what's hot, what's not, and how your company compares to our analysis of over 3,400 respondents.

Support—we're here to help

While this book is easy to follow, further follow-up questions and feedback are welcomed at any time. I would love to hear from you, even if it's just to request more statistics, be added to our mailing list, or have any streaming and digital media questions answered. If you are looking for insight on new service offerings, a recommended service provider, or have questions regarding your digital media implementation, I'll be glad to answer them. You can reach me directly at:

Dan Rayburn
www.danrayburn.com
help@danrayburn.com
(917) 523-4562

Further reading

Along with all the business information in this book, we also want to provide you with a comprehensive list of publications, Web sites, and newsletters that can provide you with additional business and technical resources on streaming and digital media subjects.

Web sites

1. StreamingMedia.com is the number one online destination for professionals seeking industry news, information, articles, directories, and services. This site features thousands of original articles, hundreds of hours of audio/video content, weekly newsletters read by over 100,000 subscribers, and a wide range of services and resources dedicated to the streaming media industry. The Web address is www.streamingmedia.com.
2. Digitalwebcast.com is Digital Media Online's home page and it serves as a hub where digital media professionals can find the tools and information they need to get their jobs done. The Web address is www.digitalwebcast.com.
3. Singingfish.com offers audio/video search services that help people easily find mp3s, movie trailers, sports highlights, newscasts, and other streaming files. The Web address is www.singingfish.com.

Newsletters

1. *Streaming Media Xtra* is a weekly e-newsletter where you can get all the breaking Streaming Media news. The Web address is www.streamingmedia.com/subscribe.asp.
2. *Stream This!* was developed exclusively for "industry" executives. The Dan Rayburn *Stream This!* monthly newsletter is *the* best compilation of news

and information for streaming media "insiders." The Web address is www.danrayburn.com.

3. *DigitalMediaWire* newsletter is considered a "must read" by industry insiders. It delivers concise and timely briefings on key business and legal and finance issues impacting digital media each business day. The Web address is www.digitalmediawire.com.

4. *DigitalMusicNews* is found on the Digital Music News Daily E-mail. The Web address is www.digitalmusicnews.com.

5. Google News Alerts are sent by e-mail when news articles appear online that match the topics you specify. The Web address is www.google.com/newsalerts.

6. Internet Acceleration is a compilation of news and events in the Internet infrastructure arena. The Web address is www.internetacceleration.com.

7. Circuits from NYTimes.com are free weekly newsletters with exclusive commentary by David Pogue, a state-of-the-art columnist. The Web address is www.nytimes.com/pages/technology/circuits/index.html.

8. *EContent Xtra* is straight from *Econtent Magazine's* news desk. The EContent Xtra e-mail newsfeed keeps you informed of events and trends driving the content industry. The Web address is www.econtentmag.com/newsletters.

Publications

1. The *Streaming Media Industry Sourcebook* is the definitive guide for implementing digital media technology and applications. The Web address is www.streamingmedia.com/sourcebook.

2. *EventDV Magazine* identifies and explains emerging digital content trends, strategies, and resources to help professionals navigate the content maze and find a clear path to profits and improved business processes. The Web address is www.eventdv.net.

CHAPTER 1

Why Get into Streaming and Digital Media?

1.1 The key question is not can you build a streaming business, but should you?

Streaming is hot, no question about it. This book is in your hands because you have some driving need, burning issue, or passing curiosity. Maybe your company has recently started a streaming project, or maybe you've been streaming for years. Perhaps you build the technologies that make streaming possible, or perhaps you are wondering what kinds of businesses, apart from adult entertainment, can possibly make money with streaming. You are not alone. Streaming has survived from its buzzword start through its blacklisted backlash to become a major movement in nearly every industry. From the obvious such as media/entertainment and financial services to the less sexy worlds of pharmaceuticals, automotive, and aerospace, digital audio and video content delivered over a network or the Internet is grabbing headlines.

Admittedly, not everyone is yelling "Full stream ahead!" The Internet is widespread, but not ever-present. Certainly farmers from Iowa to the Ukraine are using slow dial-up connections, if anything at all. Many parents and grandparents may have e-mail accounts to write to children and distant relatives, but they do not use their AOL accounts to watch movie trailers, stream Internet radio, or other more advanced streaming applications.

With that said, virtually every vertical business segment today is finding value in streaming media. Besides the Internet itself, there is no other technology which allows you to communicate more efficiently and effectively than streaming media.

1.1.1 Digital media's rapid rise

The relatively small size of the digital media technology and services market highlights the fact that streaming is still in its infancy. Depending on who you ask and which technologies you call "streaming," the market size in 2003 ranged from $800 million to $2 billion. Market forecasts for the growth rate of the digital media market over the past four years have been remarkable only for their inaccuracy. When compared to a Fortune 500 company such as Caterpillar Inc., a relatively small component of the Dow Jones Industrial Index, which reported over $4.8 billion in revenue in the first quarter of 2003 alone. This shows that digital media has a long way to go before it becomes a major market segment.

Although the market itself is small, current research indicates that the majority of enterprises have at least begun some small-scale streaming projects, and that each quarter the number of Fortune 1000 corporations setting aside a separate budget for streaming and digital media services continues to rise. In fact, a recent survey by streamingmedia.com asked corporations what they will spend on outsourced streaming media services for 2004. On average, these companies planned to broadcast 24 streaming events in the next 12 months and planned to spend an average of $104,000 on streaming technology products and services within the next year (see Figure 1.1).

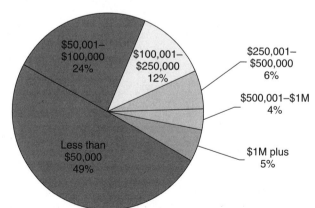

What does your organization plan to spend on streaming products technology and services over the next 12 months?

Figure 1.1: Planned spending on products/services. *(From Uses of Streaming and Digital Media report published 2004 by streamingmedia.com/Aberdeen.)*

These services are either for a narrowly focused application such as distance learning, for intermittent usage to supplementing an event such as a quarterly executive address, or for a specific audience such as an earnings call to investors. There are several non-financial or market measures to show how popular digital media is becoming. Nearly 98 percent of home consumers use a media player on a regular basis to play music and watch video clips. In mid-2004, the Web site for streamingmedia.com had tens of thousands of registered readers, and recorded upward of 1 million hits per month from corporations wanting to know more about ways to adopt streaming media solutions at their company. Apple Computer sold over 2 million single-song units at $0.99 per song within two weeks of its April 2003 launch. The legal wrangling over music and movie file sharing made weekly, and sometimes daily, headlines in major print publications from the *Wall Street Journal* and the *Herald-Tribune* to the *Economist* and *Business Week*. Niche segments of digital and streaming media entertainment, such as sites filled with sports, news, religious, and adult content, pulled in an estimated $25 billion in 2002 and 2003, and these sites were expected to grow to $400 billion by 2005. So regardless of the size, streaming is here to stay, and it is only getting more popular.

The term "streaming" itself needs to be revisited. It has become the shorthand phrase to refer to any audio and video content delivered over a network based on Internet protocols (an "IP network"). Streaming is not technically accurate. As Chapter 2 shows, streaming is only one strategy for delivering audio and video over IP networks. One accurate definition was formulated by IBM, who defined "digital media" as "unstructured content—audio, video, and images—that cannot be stored in a traditional database."[1] IBM goes on to define two major segments of digital media, one in which the media has "intrinsic value" or value that is inherent to the media itself (e.g., movies, music), and the other in which the media has "business process value," where the media becomes valuable due to the context in which it is used (e.g., training, corporate communications). Rather than continue with the streaming misnomer, this book will use "digital and streaming media" or simply "digital media" when talking about digitized audio and video on the Internet or a private intra- or extranet.

1.1.2 When technology becomes a business

Today's digital media discussions focus less on the technologies required to make digital and streaming media work, and more on the business models

---

[1] Digital Media Analyst Briefing, presented by Dick Anderson, General Manager, Digital Media Division, on May 9, 2003, in Hawthorne, New York.

required to make it successful. Debates rage about the size of the song collection required to meet the needs of a mass audience and the meaning of "fair use" as applied to digital music. Entertainment companies recognized that "inventory leakage" on an Internet scale would prevent profitability of any digital media business. In response, they attacked the degrading ethical standards of consumers with a "Be Good and Lawful" campaign around file-sharing systems. In corporations, digital media conversations focus on "cost avoidance," "cost containment," "per-user communication costs," and other business-oriented justifications.

This perspective is distinctly different from pre-2003, when the discussion was on what *could* be done at some point in the future, and what technical features and functions *would* be required to meet the demand for potential services someday. Before 1995, digital and streaming media did not exist on the Internet. The earliest content delivery network (CDN) was launched in 1996, and at that time it only delivered images and other static Web objects. Early streaming companies such as FastForward Networks and Sandpiper Networks launched in 1997 or later were either acquired by larger companies in 1999 (by Inktomi and Digital Island, respectively) or closed their doors when costs far outstripped revenue quarter after quarter.

The heyday of streaming and digital media occurred in 2000 and 2001, when new start-ups, trade periodicals, and conferences were funded by the dozen with investments from venture capital firms paranoid about missing the next big thing. Suppliers focused on small technology segments such as "on-the-fly content transcoding" and "micro-payment processing engines." Media properties such as CNN strove to provide a pervasive and consistent viewer experience. The premiere cable news network built online properties to complement, augment, and expand on its broadcast channels. The goal for CNN's online content was to equal its broadcast programming in quality, but with a diversity and interactivity possible with new media formats.

The interest in digital and streaming media followed the same curve as other technology segments. Back in 1995, in the early days of the business-oriented Internet, corporations had no choice about their Internet investments. The mantra from boardroom to back office was "Get Online—NOW!" Financial and personnel resources were thrown at the problem with abandon, because everyone was convinced that to be a winner in the Internet land grab investments must be made fast and furious.

The boom economy encouraged liberal spending with minimal financial justification. Internet equipment companies such as Cisco Systems, Sun Microsystems, and Nortel Networks grew at a phenomenal pace, and Microsoft overtook General Electric as the company with the largest stock market capitalization in the world. Cisco's market cap even briefly made it the most valuable company in the world in the last week of March 2000: With a $555 billion market cap, Cisco bested Microsoft and General Electric. A whole flock of specialized professional services companies focused on "Internet enablement services," which flew high and proud with names like Razorfish, Scient, Viant, and Zephyr.

Of course, it couldn't last. By 2002, digital and streaming media had lost its sheen because those companies selling the services were too focused on trying to have the newest and greatest technology instead of showing clients a return on their investment. Burned by the over-promising vendors and underperforming technologies, media companies and enterprises knocked digital and streaming projects to the bottom of the priority list. It didn't help that most customers of streaming and digital media technologies were struggling to remain in business themselves after a downturn in the economy and a bubonic plague of corporate malfeasance. Telecoms, service providers, and enterprises all slowed or stopped their spending on Internet infrastructure equipment and services, which bankrupted equipment providers. In mid-2003, Cisco was a much smaller fish. While General Electric had long since regained the number one spot, Cisco had shrunk down to one-quarter of its heyday size, and only one-fifth the size of an also smaller General Electric. Even Microsoft had stopped giving employees stock options as incentive, mainly because the options were no longer worth anything. The professional services firms foundered, with Razorfish, Scient, and dozens of others closing their doors or acquired for pennies on the dollar within a one-year period.

1.1.3 Out of the technology ashes and into the fiscal fire

The business model is definitely where a discussion should focus, particularly if you are trying to build a profitable business. Unlike the late 1990s, budgets are no longer limitless, and each business or project must provide a rational, justified return on investment (ROI), cost savings, or revenue model within a reasonable time frame. The discussion now is not whether a digital media service *can* be built, but in what business context *should* it be built.

While a difficult climate for vendors, the post-boom environment is actually a boon to clients and customers. The Darwinian struggle that caused the death of many fledgling technology segments has pushed the surviving vendors to develop and market products that solve real customer problems. The unjustified have had to turn around their business plans, be acquired by healthier competitors, or go out of business entirely. The result is a garage full of rapidly maturing tools just aching to be put to productive use. Content delivery networks, caching engines, payment gateways, encoding servers, and digital rights management engines are all here, many in their third or fourth generation. Moore's Innovators and Early Adopters have served their purpose by working through the difficult early period to bring technologies to maturity. Vendors who have survived through the early years may have suffered many bumps, bruises, and broken bones but now offer products that are useful to many companies. They have adopted a new means of selling and showing the value of their services and have taken the appropriate steps to use technology to help solve business problems. Digital media vendors are hearing the same message from prospective clients—that technology has no value unless it solves a business problem. It's not about the newest and greatest technology but rather whatever technology moves their business forward.

The opportunity to leverage the technology for real business solutions is here. The challenge is to learn from the experience of the past four years. This book will help you to learn how to use the mistakes made by industry vendors and early adopters to your advantage. Frank Lloyd Wright knew intimately the capabilities of the construction equipment, laborers, and materials that were available for use before he sat down to design a new structure. Philip Glass understood the range, timber, and sonic quality of musical instruments and human voices before he started composing his avant-garde symphonies. Jack Welch spent 20 years in the bowels of General Electric learning the full range of GE's many business units before repeatedly redesigning the company's mission after becoming CEO in 1981.

1.2 Using digital media for revenue generation: the value in managing your own content, channels, and customers

"Everybody else is doing it" should never be the justification for moving to a digital media system. Instead, the emphasis should be on increasing revenue or expense management. If revenue is the objective, there are three areas in which many companies use digital media: content monetization, channel control, and customer conversion. These are all concerned with building top-line sales, either through the sale of the digital media itself or by using the digital media to increase the sale of cars, dishwashers, detergent, or other products.

1.2.1 Content monetization

Any company with digital audio or video that has intrinsic value should be building a digital media strategy to sell, or "monetize," that content over the Internet. The nature of digital media is that it does not degrade over time and that an infinite number of copies can be made from an original without affecting the quality of the original. The nature of the Internet is that any point can be accessed by another point, that it is pervasive and redundant, and that it is quickly becoming more akin to a utility resource like natural gas and electricity than a jumble of technologies. When combined, digital media plus the Internet means that an audio or video file with intrinsic value could be sold and delivered directly to anyone in the world with an Internet connection—more potential customers than could ever fit into even the largest of retail stores. By 2004 80 percent of the total population had access to the Internet from any location, up from 75 percent in the Arbitron/Edison Media Research survey done in January 2003. The number of Americans with residential broadband Internet access has tripled since January 2001, rising to 48 million as of April 2004.[2]

Aside from selling popular content to millions of people, the Internet's reach also makes it feasible to begin selling niche content to small, specific groups. NASCAR racing has a large enough following to merit cable television broadcasts, but locomotive enthusiasts may be just as willing to pay to see footage of a Garratt locomotive crossing the North Fork Trestle outside of North Conway, New Hampshire. The potential is for anyone with content that is valuable to any group should be able to sell that content via the Internet. There are many technical issues to understand when designing a content monetization business model, and it is a key objective of almost every chapter in this book.

1.2.2 Channel control

Any media and entertainment company operating today is looking to augment their existing distribution channels with the Internet. Some are even trying to circumvent their current distribution channels entirely. Movie and television production currently relies on local affiliates and cable television operators to get their content out to the public. Retail stores such as Wal-Mart, Blockbuster, and amazon.com are the main avenues for customers to purchase music and video content.

Content producers and owners have seen the Internet as an avenue to regain control over the distribution channel. The Internet itself is collectively

---

[2] Source: eMarketert.com, Broadband Worldwide 2004: Subscriber Update report (April, 2004).

owned and operated by over 9,000 different service providers, so that the content owner does not need to be beholden to any single service provider as a channel partner. Going direct to the customer can remove the wholesale costs and increase the average selling price of any individual product. Unlike distribution of physical goods, given that the content is digital, there are few efficiencies to be gained in terms of inventory holdings: The costs to hold the inventory do not change significantly from the costs to store the assets and intellectual property. However, channel management, co-marketing, and other fees associated with supporting a distribution partnership can be avoided.

The basic technology for digital and streaming media has been developed. Now new distribution agreements with other channel partners need to be negotiated. The Internet has the potential to overtake the traditional modes, but it is only a small part of today's distribution, and no distributor will sit idly by as the world changes. Cable television companies are proactively encouraging legislation to prevent telecom companies from becoming content distributors. They are also using their current clout to secure windows to capture the value of video on-demand via the cable set-top box. Blockbuster and other rental chains are including assumptions about Internet delivery of films to coincide when DVDs hit the shelves versus on-demand content. And, of course, the Recording Industry Association of America (RIAA) is aggressively targeting file sharing at the software, service provider, and individual levels. As outlined in the beginning, these are all business discussions. It's not "Can we do it?" but "Now that we can, how do we control its impact on our existing revenue streams?"

1.2.3 Customer contact

The goal of marketing is to be able to tailor messages to the specific needs of each potential customer. Companies must rely on statistical sampling, focus groups, and market studies, mainly because they have no direct contact with most customers. The distributors see the customers' faces, record the customers' purchasing habits, and charge content owners for the privilege of accessing that information.

Direct distribution means the content owner would have access to that unbiased and raw information. Unmediated interactions also allow content owners to have one-to-one marketing with the customers and to control which products and services are associated with what sales process. The result is that while some level of abstraction will continue to be required, either through a distributor or other third-party information collection agency, direct customer contact is often reason enough to adopt a digital media distribution system. Understanding the capabilities of data collection and using that knowledge in negotiations with distributors could radically alter the distribution landscape over the next three years.

1.3 Using digital media to reduce costs and increase communication: leveraging digital media for different applications

The other side of the coin is internal usage, or using digital media to cut the cost of doing business. The below-the-line impact can be divided into four categories: telecommunication expenses, customer service, time to market, and information quality. With the exception of telecom expenses, these uses make a difference to the organization when audio and video is part of a larger application or business process, and not a stand-alone solution in itself.

1.3.1 Telecommunication expense

The most popular use of streaming media is to replace other forms of video communication with IP video. Many firms have two or three separate networks in place: voice, video, and data. By moving to digital media, the video network can be eliminated along with all the maintenance, management, and support costs associated with it. Research shows a trend over the next few years toward "convergence" of voice, video, and data onto the same network. The ROI for the IP network would be accelerated, and the overall telecommunication expense for the company decreases. As digital ecosystems begin to emerge, many types of digital media technologies, which once operated separately, will soon have the ability to work with one another in a seamless model. Companies who have adopted streaming video technology say they use it to make their internal communication efforts more efficient and to reach more employees on a near simultaneous basis. This is done more cheaply than traditional means of communication. As shown in Figure 1.2, small, medium, and large companies can all benefit from the technology.

With a broadly deployed IP video infrastructure, companies can move executive communications, company training, regulatory compliance, and other video-intensive activities onto the corporate network. Corporations used to have a policy against moving digital media over the company backbone due to the size of the files and the sustained rate of delivery, which

Hang Up and Stream
Corporate communications using streaming–based services vs.
phone–based services

COMPANY SIZE	SAMPLE APPLICATION	MODE	PARTICIPANTS	COST
Small (200 employees)	Product Demonstration	Telephone[1] Streamed[2]	40	$960.00 $5.76
Medium (1,500 employees)	Product Demonstration or Investor Relations Call	Telephone Streamed	150	$3,600.00 $21.60
Large (10,000 employees)	Investor Relations Call	Telephone Streamed	500	$12,000.00 $72.00

[1]Assumes a real-time conference call cost of 40 cents per minute. [2]Assumes a bit rate of 16 Kbps at a rate of $0.0024 per minute. Source: RHR.

Figure 1.2: Using Streaming for cost savings. *(From Jupiter Media Metrix, Effective Enterprise Uses for Streaming.)*

either slowed or stopped other more important business applications. Chapters 2 and 5 show that, by learning from some object lessons of the base, this potential side effect can be minimized or avoided entirely.

1.3.2 Customer service

Some studies show that, compared to the cost of $25 per call to a live person, the cost for an automated customer service can fall as low as $2.50. As if a tenfold cost savings per call is not enough, Web-based customer service is accessible 24 hours a day to anyone in the world. The problem has been that some products or services are too complex to explain in a document or hypertext format. For example, the Apple iPod is relatively straightforward for anyone who is reasonably adept at using the Internet. However, as Apple expands its market to include less tech-savvy individuals, it will begin to experience customer service calls with the same frequently asked questions: How do I plug it into my computer? Why can't I find The Beatles on the song list? How do I edit my song descriptions?

Palm Computers, the makers of the PalmPilot personal digital assistants (PDAs), experienced this problem in 2001 and 2002. As the company worked to sustain PDA sales, it expanded into new customer segments. Customer service representatives would spend anywhere from five to fifteen minutes on the phone with customers in setup and problem-solving sessions.

The digital media answer to this problem was the short video demo, which visually depicted how to install and configure the PalmPilots. When new customers called, their need was determined and they were directed to the appropriate video on the customer service site. After this, call time dropped to less than two minutes per call, and not only did customer support costs decrease, but customer satisfaction improved.

Palm Computers had to consider the costs of creating, delivering, and managing the digital media when designing its customer support site. It ended up using a combination of CDNs and managed delivery technologies to move the video efficiently and collect information on customer usage of the videos. One of the case studies at the end of this chapter highlights how Starbucks is using streaming media to sell more products and communicate more efficiently with its customers via the Internet.

1.3.3 Information quality

The quality of information conveyed by visual and audio content can be better, or it can be worse, than written information. Certainly, though, the quality is different. For some types of content, one-inch-square playback is sufficient. For other types, full-screen DVD quality is required. Due to the way streaming media compression technology works, content that has a lot of movement, such as sports-related content, needs more bandwidth to be able to deliver more frames per second, which equals a higher quality video experience. Yet for other video content, such as a speech from a podium where only a talking head is seen, an acceptable finished product with less bandwidth can be achieved because there is no need to deliver as many frames of video. Also, the value of an audio stream for investor relations calls, radio broadcasts, and text-to-speech applications in most cases fulfills the end user's need without the use of video. The type of digital media delivered is based solely on the type of content, the quality expectations, and the technical limitations of the end users receiving the digital media.

For any company using digital media, the revenue and expense impact are not mutually exclusive. A company is not limited to just one or two areas of benefit. From top-line revenue to bottom-line expense management, any company can push into the full range of benefits of using digital media internally or externally. In fact, to gain the most advantage from a digital media system, companies should look to existing leverage or new investments across as many areas as possible. Content developed for outward-facing customer sales promotion can also be re-purposed for the customer service section of the Web site as well as for field sales support. The caching infrastructure initially deployed to move the CEO's Monday morning address from New York to the 100 locations worldwide can also be used for distance learning, product briefings, and other visually intensive activities. Current research shows that most digital media systems are deployed within a

Product Launches, Sales Training Will Lead Application Categories

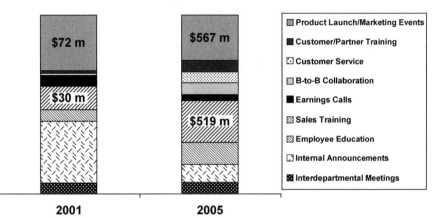

Figure 1.3: Use of business streaming and media applications. *(From Jupiter Media Metrix, Effective Enterprise Uses for Streaming.)*

company to support a specific application, and as seen in Figure 1.3, product launches and sales training will soon be the leading applications.

The ROI for the project expense, though, can be greatly accelerated if its use is spread to other applications or groups within the organization. Chapter 7 and the case studies at the end of each chapter should give some ideas about where to look beyond the first application of a digital media system within an organization.

1.4 Early successes show big returns if they're done right

1.4.1 Case study: Starbucks

Starbucks was seeking a creative way to further engage its online customers with its products, company, and brand in order to maximize awareness of sales opportunities. Because online shoppers do not have immediate access to a sales associate, Starbucks needed a better way to explain the features, benefits, and usability of its more complicated offerings. In looking for a marketing solution to solve this challenge, Starbucks discovered Vendaria (vendaria.com), a company that provides an easy-to-implement way for companies to use digital media in e-commerce merchandising, banner ads, and e-mail marketing campaigns.

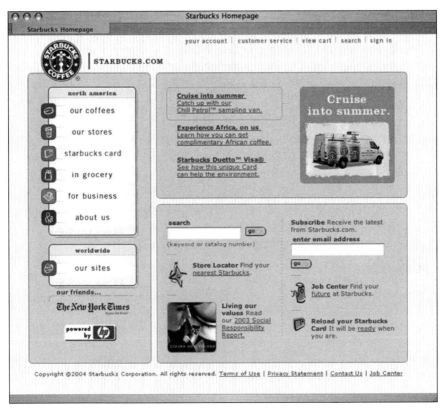

Figure 1.4: *www.starbucks.com*

Starbucks used the Vendaria's digital media marketing solutions (Figure 1.4) to enhance its online shopping experience and was initially attracted to these solutions for making the end user's experience easy. Starbucks product videos can be viewed by consumers with all modem speeds including dial-up, which is the majority of the population, by bringing them video quality equal to those with a broadband connection while using digital media technology that does not require the user to download a media player. This makes it easy for the most inexperienced computer user to view the product videos. These videos allow Starbucks to better explain the multiple features of its brewing equipment in a way that is easier for the consumer to understand and more engaging than copy or static images alone. This enables Starbucks to have better interaction with their online audience and to provide ongoing education to qualified, interested customers. This ultimately drives higher sales for those products. Leveraging yet another channel with the videos, Starbucks implemented video-enabled banner ads on MSN.com. This allowed the company to target a much broader audience with eye-catching rich-media ads intended to drive interested customers to the Starbucks Web site. Starbucks also sent a video-enhanced e-mail to its subscriber list enabling Starbucks to deliver intricate sales messages to a prequalified audience of potential buyers leading them straight to the product detail page.

In just a short time frame, Starbucks saw an increased awareness of visitors to their Web site. This helped drive sales of Starbucks brewing equipment higher as well as providing an enhanced user experience through the inclusion of rich media. The digital media strategy of Starbucks has led to a significantly higher number of conversions from clicks to buys.

1.4.2 Case study: New England Cable News (NECN)

Eager to leverage the Internet as a communication channel, New England Cable News (NECN) needed an effective digital media solution that would enable the company to seamlessly bring its cable broadcasts to life online without making a large infrastructure investment. The company's vision was to provide viewers with around-the-clock, high-quality online access to up-to-date news, weather, entertainment, and sports video clips. It was important that the technology behind NECN's site mirror the top-notch performance of its offline broadcasts, make the online experience as enjoyable as watching television, and help strengthen NECN's brand awareness.

Launched in 1992, NECN is the largest regional cable news channel in the country, serving 2.8 million households in over 820 New England communities. The station covers breaking news stories as well as weather, sports, and entertainment 24 hours a day. In 1996, NECN introduced its Web site (Figure 1.5) and became the pioneer in streaming video for news coverage. The Web site provides continual access to broadcast streaming videos with over 1,000 news-related clips available per month to its online viewing audience of 150,000 people. There is no doubt that the growing popularity of the Internet as a news source, especially during the workday, has contributed to NECN's success as the premiere Web destination for New England video news coverage.

NECN realized that in order to strengthen its reputation as a dependable New England news source, its Web site needed to deliver uninterrupted, high-quality streaming clips that reflected the integrity of the news station. As the popularity of the Web as a news source grew, the NECN site needed to handle unexpected traffic spikes, which have been known to triple the number of

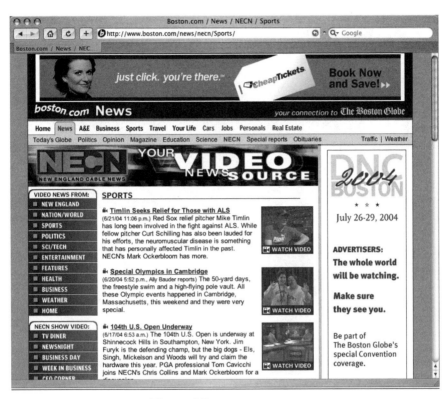

Figure 1.5: *www.necn.com*

visits and videos streamed, as a result of major breaking news, within seconds. It was necessary for the station to find a cost-effective technology solution that could reliably deliver high-quality content around-the-clock. This technology was digital media.

NECN chose an outsourced video on-demand solution from Mirror Image (www.mirror-image.com) to cost effectively handle its streaming media needs based on their scalability, reliability, and ability to support multiple streaming media formats. In addition, the solution offered NECN the ability to immediately upload content and gave them greater management intelligence on viewership patterns and bandwidth usage. By removing the "heavy lifting" from NECN's origin server, the streaming media service also empowered the station to focus on its core business without additional infrastructure overhead. Up and running in a day, the outsourced provider worked with NECN to seamlessly integrate the solution and automate the upload, publishing, and distribution process of files to meet specific requirements. The moment

Figure   1.6: *NECN's   immediate   streaming   delivery   to   users.   (From www.necn.com.)*

NECN transfers files to Mirror Image, they are automatically distributed to Mirror Image's network and available for immediate streaming delivery to users (Figure 1.6). This new digital media solution prepared NECN to easily handle the overwhelming traffic due to the catastrophic events of September 11, 2001. NECN surpassed most news broadcasting performance abilities that day, and provided their audience with the immediate insight others could not. As a result, video on-demand solutions such as this enable e-businesses like NECN to cost effectively maximize the bottom line.

By working on their digital content delivery strategy for the last two years, NECN has become a top-notch news site, with an incredible performance track record of delivering over 150,000 news-related streamed clips per month. In fact, frequent NECN visitors have commented on the site's enhanced performance and better overall experience, and NECN is developing ways to reap the benefits from better online advertising. Because of their digital media strategy, NECN is now able to focus on developing profitable partnerships with other top New England news sites such as boston.com, the city's online version of the major daily newspaper, the *Boston Globe*. NECN is currently in the process of adding a video component to boston.com, which would create an evolutionary video-integrated site with streaming audio and video. This "next-generation site" is expected to increase customer activity and viewer growth and traffic while helping to set the stage for future revenue opportunities. With the video on-demand solution, NECN offers viewers streaming news feeds that are as reliable and as enjoyable as watching TV. Because of digital media technology, they are able to partner with boston.com and continue on this path to reach their goal as the leader in streaming video for news coverage. By implementing a digital video on-demand solution, NECN has enjoyed benefits that included saving 55% on reduced infrastructure and proposed operating costs, enhanced site performance as a result of faster downloads of over 150,000 clips per month, and the ability to expand business opportunities to include partnerships with Web sites like boston.com.

CHAPTER 2

Technology Primer: The Basics of Streaming and Digital Media

2.1 Introduction to streaming and digital media technologies

This chapter introduces streaming and digital media technologies, defines the technical differences between the types of content commonly delivered over the Internet, and highlights the key differences between traditional broadcasting and Internet technologies. Skip this chapter if, when asked by a colleague, customer, or cousin, you can confidently explain *all* of the following:

- The basic technical concepts of digital media delivery, such as streaming, download, loss, latency, jitter, content delivery networks (CDNs), and digital rights management (DRM)
- The difference between the two Internet media delivery approaches—streaming and download—and how those strategies create live, simulated live, and on-demand media playback
- The cost models to scale traditional broadcasting media and Internet media delivery when building a service to reach a few hundred, a few thousand, or hundreds of thousands of consumers and users
- The three metrics on which consumers and users evaluate "content quality" for Internet delivery
- The five strategies currently used to secure content delivery over the Internet to public and private audiences

Understanding these five areas is essential for building a solid digital media business. If you already understand these points, then jump to Chapter 3, The Four Keys to a Profitable Streaming or Digital Media Business. This chapter builds on these concepts and delves into more detail about how businesses can capitalize on the scalability, quality, security, and audience measurement capability of digital media.

By the end of this chapter, you will be able to explain the broad basics of digital media technology to your boss over coffee or your mother over Christmas dinner.

2.1.1 Internet basics: built for reliability, not quality

A quick overview of the Internet in general is required before learning about streaming and digital media. Although it may seem that the Internet leapt fully formed from a collective consciousness in the early 1990s, it actually began as a project of the U.S. government and MIT in the early 1970s. Called ARPANET, it was the first attempt to connect computers across the country, and eventually around the world, into a loose community of interrelated processing centers. ARPANET's objective was to build a fully redundant and fully reliable communication system that would operate even in the event of a catastrophic global crisis such as nuclear war or a meteor hitting the Earth. "Networking" is a common word used to describe social gatherings, job hunting, and computer systems, but the concept didn't exist before ARPANET.

In ARPANET and subsequently the Internet, all communications occur in a packet-based system: Data, files, and digital objects are chunked up into subsets of the whole and wrapped in digital packets. These packets are then sent over the network using standardized protocols such as hypertext transfer protocol (HTTP) and file transfer protocol (FTP). These protocols employ a series of query-response and try-retry transactions where information is stored and used.

When you click on a hotlink, your Web browser finds where the information is stored using a universal record locator (URL) number and the domain name system (DNS), which connects the www.danrayburn.com to the computer location http://1113622038. When a request is made, the protocols send a list of numbers that represent all the packets the requesting computer expects to receive. The content origin, where the content is stored, starts sending numbered packets that correspond to the list. The requester gets them one at a time, in no particular sequence, and reassembles the packets back into the original file.

If a specific packet is missing, the requesting computer sends out another request for the missing data. The requester tries and retries until all the packets are received or until a preset amount of time passes. At this point, the requesting computer displays a "file not found" or "server too busy" notice. When the globe icon spins away in the upper right-hand corner of Microsoft Internet Explorer, the try-retry process is occurring. Packets can be lost during the transfer process for any number of reasons, which will be discussed shortly. In fact, the Internet was designed with the assumption that packets would be lost regularly, as the industry loss average is 1 in 12. When you get a red "X" instead of a picture, the delivery has failed. Clicking the refresh icon will repeat the whole process, sometimes filling in the X. The user can then decide whether to make do with the received information, initiate a new round of requests, or give up all together.

If that doesn't sound reliable, it's because it's not. The Internet isn't reliable like turning on a light switch, which approaches 100 percent reliability for the 100-year-old technology. The builders of ARPANET and the Internet were not trying to create a system that would deliver every single packet every single time. Instead, they created an architecture that built in the assumption that any individual transaction can fail, and yet the overall network could still function. It places the responsibility on the requesting computer to confirm if everything has been received and to track what has or has not been received. The requesting computer can seek out alternate paths to the origin or even other sources of the same information.

If a particular path goes down, the requester can try a new path. No individual path becomes a single point of failure for the overall network. Theoretically each path is as good as another. With a large enough network that has enough alternate paths, the overall network itself should never fail. During the 9/11 crisis, when the phone system on the entire East Coast crashed due to suddenly oversubscribed circuits and key telecom hubs in lower Manhattan were lost, the Internet slowed down but never stopped. E-mails took longer than usual to go through, but it was a difference of a few minutes versus the usual few seconds. Information requests were rerouted around the world, served from temporary stores or "caches," and communication continued. The same is not true for telephone service: All carriers were out of operation for a period ranging from hours to days.

In the late 1980s and early 1990s, several major computer industry trends intersected to make the Internet more than just a science experiment or military project:

- Personal computers (PCs) began to be produced in mass quantities, which dropped the average price so that anyone could buy one.

- Following Moore's Law,[1] computing power crossed a critical threshold during this period, which provided powerful processing capabilities in a small, affordable form factor as Intel released the 386 and 486 microprocessors.
- Apple and Microsoft released the Macintosh and Windows 3.0 operating systems, respectively, which significantly simplified PC usage for the average office user or home consumer.
- Desktop productivity software hit the market, which presented a productivity-enhancing reason for businesses and individuals to purchase PCs.
- IBM, Novell, and other companies developed networking software, which allowed multiple PCs to share printers, storage, and other network resources.
- In 1993 the first Web browser, Mosaic, was widely adopted. It used hypertext markup language (HTML) to wrap HTTP, FTP, and other protocols into an easy-to-use and visually appealing wrapper around HTTP on Internet protocols.

Due to these advances, the Internet consists of thousands of large and small networks connected together. At one point, there were over 12,000 registered networks contributing resources to the Internet, not counting individual users or unregistered networks. Those networks themselves consist of hundreds or thousands of individual machines. Service providers with thousands of servers and millions of miles of copper wire and fiber optic cables, the "pipes" through which the packets travel, lease usage at generally affordable levels. Universities, corporations, government offices, and individuals all contribute resources to the great Internet cloud.

2.1.2 Static versus streaming at the content level

Until the late 1990s, all content on the Internet was static. Static content, in this context, refers to information that is created and formatted in advance, made available for consumption, and then fully transferred to a consumer or a user's PC before it is used. For example, the typical Web page has static content in the form of text, logos, images, and advertisements. Static content also includes individual files such as word processing documents and spread-

---

[1] Alan Moore, founder of Intel, theorized that the number of capacitors that could fit on a silicon chip, and therefore the computing power of the chip, would double every 18 to 24 months. A corollary to Moore's Law is that the price of silicon chips would be cut in half every 18 months as well. Moore's rough estimate has held remarkably true since the mid-1970s.

sheets. It could also refer to a copy of a large database of customer information that is being duplicated from New York to Idaho as a redundant backup.

Static content should generally be delivered as quickly as possible, but once delivered, it doesn't require that an open connection be maintained to the Internet. As discussed above, when a user enters a domain name or clicks on a URL, the Web browser sends a request for the Web page, information is transferred from the source server to the user's desktop, and the Web page appears in the browser. Once the transfer is complete, the connection to the Internet is dormant and unused, or "off," until the next Web page is requested.

Some elements are animated within the Web browser, but technically they are also static content. For example, a rotating CNN logo is a discrete file that is fully transferred to the user's computer, typically in the form of an animated "GIF" before being activated. The same can be true for assets that are developed in Flash, an application from Macromedia. Flash objects can be highly dynamic in appearance, but have been traditionally downloaded before they are used. In early 2004, Macromedia announced a new suite of Flash servers that also supports true live streaming.

Video and audio can also be delivered in this fashion. In a download-then-play model, an audio or video file is completely transferred to the requesting computer before the movie or sound stream is initiated. In this model, digital audio and video are handled like a duplicate customer database by the network resources in the Internet.

There are two potential problems with delivering video and audio files as if they were the same as static content:

1. File size: Audio/video files are much larger than most commonly used files. The CNN logo is less than 4 kilobytes (KB) in size, whereas a 30-minute VCR-quality video can exceed 300 megabytes (MB) and a full-length movie over 3 gigabytes (GB). In other words, audio and video can be a hundred to a thousand times larger than the average Web page. The transfer time for this file size even over a high-speed cable modem or fast Ethernet network is measured in hours, not seconds. Users must wait for the information to become usable.
2. File value: Audio/video files often have a much higher inherent value than commonly used static files. Audio and video content is expensive to create or has an associated artistic value. Because the files are stored on the destination machine, content owners risk theft and illegal sharing by users. The content can then be altered or the monetary value diluted. The importance of content security is directly tied to the value of the content. Movie

trailers are freely available to anyone, and security strategies are designed to prevent content alteration. For copyright-protected or high-value content, security strategies focus on limiting access to ensure that proper fees are collected or that competitors do not gain access to sensitive information.

The security issue is not trivial. In 2001, there were few options to prevent users from duplicating, distributing, or altering the downloaded audio and video once it was completely transferred to a user's machine. The poster child of this problem was Napster, a distributed file-sharing service that allowed anyone to trade digital music files. The end result, after years of litigation, was Napster shut down by court order in March 2002[2] for infringing on copyright laws. The U.S. Court of Appeals for the 9th Circuit decided that, due to immature technology, Napster was unable to effectively filter out illegally distributed files. The damage was already done: The decision came after tens of millions of songs had been traded without compensating the record industry or the artists.

2.1.3 Enter streaming media

Streaming media is a strategy to help jump the hurdles of file size and file value for audio and video content. Rather than transfer information to users' computers (in the streaming industry it is referred to as a "progressive download"), it is more like television: The audio or video data are played as they are received and no data are transferred permanently to the user's computer.

Streaming overcomes the file size problem because, with streaming, users can begin to consume the media as it is received. A 600-MB file starts playing once a sufficient amount of data are transferred into a media player's temporary storage, called a cache or "buffer." The content then looks like any television or radio signal, as images and sound play out on the computer desktop.

Streaming also addresses content security. Content owners can collect fees for content usage by setting up payment gateways at the beginning of the stream. Once access is granted, the stream starts. As a general rule, content owners don't need to worry about consumers or users copying or distributing the files because the users store nothing on their machines to copy or distribute. Although there are a few shareware programs available on the underground market that *can* capture and save a video stream, the tools are not mainstream, nor are they expected to be anytime soon. Only highly sophisticated users have the knowledge or equipment to capture and retransmit the stream.

---

[2] Napster Copyright Litigation, U.S. Court of Appeals for the 9th Circuit, March 25, 2002.

2.1.4 Streaming across the Internet

While streaming media does increase security and enable delivery of large files, it also imposes a significant delivery cost to the network. As shown in Figure 2.1, the Internet infrastructure of the content delivery value chain can be segmented into four separate regions. The First Mile includes all the equipment where the information is stored, such as databases, servers, data center infrastructure, and access connections. The Internet Cloud, or Middle Mile, refers to the vast interconnect networks that make up the Internet, such as thousands of service provider transport pipes, routers, and switches, and other invisible peering points of the Internet. The Internet Edge is actually not a real "edge," but refers to the point at which a home consumer or business user connects to the Internet at large. The Last Mile denotes the local access connection between the user and the Internet Edge.

Behind the scenes, streaming media requires a continuous connection between the viewer and the content source. Unlike static content, the normal state of the network connection between end user and content source is "on": A link is engaged, and network resources and bandwidth are used until the stream ends or is disconnected. To smooth playback, most streaming media players temporarily store a portion of the content in the

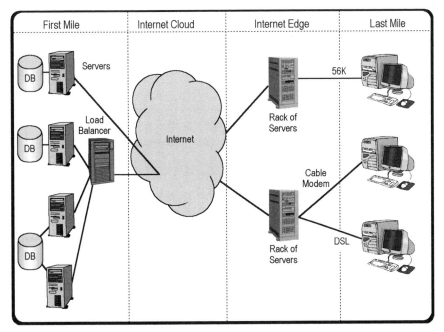

Figure 2.1: *The content delivery value chain.*

buffer, caching anywhere from a few seconds to a few minutes depending on the technology.

The "always on" connection between the user and the content source means that a constant, steady connection must exist between the source site and the end-user's player. Because this is computer technology, the network rarely (if ever) works perfectly. Therefore, there are a host of problems that continually occur in the Internet to prevent a constant, steady connect. Network outages, congestion, or delays at any link in the chain can interrupt playback. The types of interference are generally classified into three areas: latency, loss, and re-buffering.

1. Latency: Due to standard Internet protocols, there is an inherent delay, or latency, when a piece of information is requested and when it is delivered. The latency mainly affects the amount of time a user must wait to see the information. In the case of streaming media, latency impacts when a consumer or user can start watching the video. The more network connections, or "hops," that must be traveled between the requester and the origin, and the larger the file requested, the longer the start-up latency. Some authorization and security systems in the First Mile may also increase latency.

2. Loss: Routers, switches, caches, and other network equipment are designed to handle a specific number of simultaneous transactions. If the equipment exceeds its limit, information packets are dropped entirely from the network. The assumption is that the user's machine will use a try-retry approach of transmission control protocol (TCP)/IP to repeat the request for a missing packet. This approach does not affect static content delivery, except to slow it down. For streaming, though, packet loss translates into skipped frames, missing audio, or stopped playback.

3. Re-buffering: Consistency is key in delivering streaming media. The media player's buffer compensates for some variability by providing a local cache of information. Measuring the rate at which packets are received, the player calculates how much information to buffer before starting playback. A slow but constant connection causes a long buffering period before start-up but would not affect playback quality once it begins. Players can't compensate if the rate changes once playback starts, and, once the cache is empty, playback stops. Any number of issues can cause the transfer rate to change during playback. Re-buffering refers to a changing transfer rate, which then results in jumpy or stopped playback.

When faced with missing data due to loss, latency, or re-buffering, the media player either stops playback or skips over that segment, presenting the end user with an erratic audio and poor quality video experience.

2.1.5 Internet distance does not equal geographic distance

With digital media, the Internet distance doesn't equal geographic distance. Whether on the public Internet, a private intranet, or a local area network (LAN), the distance between two physical points is rarely a network straight line. A user in Peoria, Illinois, accessing amazon.com may get the information from Seattle, Washington, where Amazon is based. However, to get from Peoria to Seattle, the Internet border gateway protocol (BGP) may route the user through Atlanta, Georgia; Dallas, Texas; *and* Denver, Colorado.

Thus, geographical mileage is only one component of distance, but often not the most important one. In 2003, the average Internet distance between a requesting user's location and the content's stored location was between 7 and 14 network connection hops. International connections can take significantly more. At any network hop, traffic could be slowed down, held up, or stopped all together. With static content, the variability is not much of a problem. Assuming the information is available either at the primary location or elsewhere, Internet protocols will re-request the missing information until it is fulfilled or until a certain amount of time elapses. There may be a delay, but the content gets through.

Streaming media is not as tolerant of network delays as static content, primarily because the overriding qualification for streaming delivery is not speed of download. A 30-minute video cannot be viewed in 20 minutes. Instead, streaming media requires constant bandwidth availability and consistent connection reliability during transmission. As shown in Figure 2.2, there are five areas where providers of technologies and services have improved the capability for delivering streaming media:

1. Higher content quality: Content owners must balance playback quality with delivery costs and performance constraints. New encoding/decoding formats, or "codecs," are allowing content owners to do more with less, but there is still a long way to go before the bit rate, frame size, and other aspects of playback are comparable to television quality video.
2. Better servers in the First Mile: Internet service providers (ISPs) and content providers increase the serving rate and simultaneous user capacity of their servers or supplement their networks with streaming-capable caches to meet the volume of incoming streaming requests.
3. Greater backbone bandwidth in the Internet Cloud: Larger network pipes have been installed to the point where some analysts predict that the fiber will rot in the ground before it is ever fully used. In addition, bandwidth allocation technologies allow service providers and enterprises to cordon

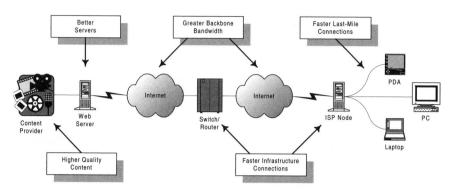

Figure 2.2: *Internet bottlenecks for content delivery. (From Michael Hoch,* Understanding the Technology of Digital Media: A "Streaming" Primer, *June 2003, Aberdeen Group.)*

off segments of any specific bandwidth link for a specific application, such as streaming media. Traffic shapers can't control bandwidth usage over the entire connection between the viewer and the content source, only the links to which they are attached. However, they do help the backbone itself meet the stringent streaming requirements.

4. Faster infrastructure connections in the First Mile, Internet Cloud, and Internet Edge: A large bandwidth pipe was only half the battle. The Internet junctions of routers, switches, etc., have also been upgraded to be capable of consistent 500 Kbps or greater per user data transmission.

5. Faster Last Mile connections: This is probably the largest inhibitor technically. In response, users have gradually adopted digital subscriber lines (DSL) and high-speed cable modem services for connections faster than dial-up access can provide. With a theoretical maximum of 56.6 Kbps, dial-up services are too slow to deliver even low-quality streaming media. In early 2004, broadband reached the major milestone of 100 million subscribers globally. Because subscribers include residential and business accounts, the actual number of users is far greater, roughly 250 million to date, a total that will near 300 million by Q1 of 2005.[3]

Security is also a critical feature. It is so important that it will be addressed in greater detail later in this chapter and in subsequent chapters. At a high level, digital rights management (DRM) technologies have improved the speed of authorization at a streaming gateway, and have also made down-

---

[3] Source: eMarketert.com, Broadband Worldwide 2004: Subscriber Update report (April 2004).

load-then-play a viable option. Encryption technology prevents use of files unless the user acquires a unique, registered key or digital certificate, which would then bind the media with a specific physical machine. It is extremely difficult to decrypt the file without a key or to use an encrypted file on a different computer without first receiving a key from the content owner. Most DRM applications use 128-bit encryption or higher. The first 64-bit decryption was completed in September 2002, but only after 4 years of 24-hour-a-day processing by over 330,000 computers.[4]

2.2 Technical variations of Internet media from traditional broadcasting

It is important to understand the differences between traditional technology and the technology that powers the Internet, streaming, and downloaded content delivery. "Traditional" in this case includes nearly every distribution channel available to move audio and video content from where it is created and/or stored to where it is consumed. The most obvious channel is traditional broadcasting, where content is delivered via transmission towers and cable operators over wavelengths and frequencies. Broadcasting includes such public applications as radio and television programming. Traditional models also include the private broadcast of audio and video, such as closed-circuit TV, corporate television channels, remote training facilities, etc. Finally, traditional models can also include distribution of audio and video on physical media, such as compact discs, cassette tapes, videotapes, and digital video discs.

In this context, those who work behind the Internet intend to replace anything traditional with a network-based technology or service. There are several strong and proven reasons for wanting to replace traditional delivery models with Internet delivery. These include:

- Speed benefits such as faster time to market and shorter production cycle times
- Cost benefits, such as lower distribution costs, lower marketing costs, and lower customer service costs
- Improved customer quality through direct-to-consumer marketing, increased reach to new audiences and geographic regions, and the ability to gather granular customer usage data

---

[4] Distributed Team Collaborates to Solve Secret Key Challenge, *RSA Security,* September 26, 2002.

- New application benefits, such as small-audience programming for entertainment or corporate usage and other types of art, entertainment, or applications that were not previously economically feasible or technically possible

The speed benefits are readily understandable. Because any location on the Internet is accessible from almost any other location, Internet distribution avoids physical inhibitors such as the time it takes to duplicate, package, ship, unload, stock, select, and purchase the content. Content can be delivered from the origin to the user as quickly as the Internet can carry it. For private distribution, the expectation is that video over networks will become as ubiquitous as voice over a network, and that a video conversation will be as easy as a phone call.

2.3 The fundamental difference in cost structures between the old and new

The costs benefits and the quality differences between the old and the new models are not as easily understood. Setting aside the quality discussion, both models require upfront costs to develop and format the content. These costs may change in the Internet world, but in the current environment, most content development processes are not changing. Studio space, production houses, creative teams, and artists, as well as other costs involved in creating movie, music, advertising, corporate, and personal content are still in place. A host of technological tools are rapidly developing to help these areas, but that discussion is beyond the boundaries of this book.

The distribution, delivery, and customer/user support costs are drastically different between traditional models and the Internet world. Both have fixed and variable costs, but the relative weight of fixed versus variable is significant. In a traditional model, content owners are heavily weighted toward fixed distribution costs. These costs include physical broadcasting facilities, such as capturing and encoding facilities; licensing and transmission costs for wavelengths and channels; and maintenance and storage costs.

2.3.1 Traditional broadcasting cost structures are heavy on fixed, low on variable

The fixed costs to run a television or radio station for a specific region or for a closed-circuit television system for internal corporate use increases by specific steps. Initial start-up costs include reaching a specific geographic audience, either due to the transmission radius of a broadcasting tower or the licensing agreements with a given cable television provider. WBCN in Boston is an alternative radio station broadcasting to 4.5 million listeners within the major Boston metropolitan area. The station has two towers in three locations around the region, which gives WBCN a broadcast radius of about 20 miles. Nielsen/Arbitron statistics show that WBCN has a 7.2 rating, which indicates that, out of the 4.5 million potential listeners, the station has an average of 300,000 listeners.

It is difficult to calculate the expense to set up a similar station. Because WBCN has built its broadcast network gradually over the past 25 years, the costs today would differ significantly from what WBCN actually spent. Those costs would not be transferable to other regions either, because frequency licenses are priced by metro region and real estate in Boston is much more expensive than real estate in Nebraska.

However, assume that the fixed start-up costs are sunk: They are over and done with, currently appearing in the company's financial statements as a debt liability against which payments are made on a predictable schedule. The main variable cost is the per-user cost whereby the station pays royalties to content owners based on the number of users within the geographic region. The fees vary based on the content's popularity, the station's listener base (size, demographics, etc.), the number of content plays, and the negotiation strength of the station with the content owner. WBCN's primary income, advertising revenue, is also per-user dependent, which is driven by the station's listener base and its negotiation strength with advertisers. As long as the incoming ad revenue covers three things—the outgoing royalties, the existing debt that represents the sunk costs, and the fixed costs of running the station (including sales, general, and administrative costs)—WBCN is profitable. Even as part of a large, multichannel operator such as Clear Channel, each station within the overall operation is accountable for profitability along these lines. Television broadcasting has a similar business model, with the added level of cable operator distribution costs that supplement or replace the broadcast tower.

What happens if WBCN wants to increase revenue? The most direct way is increase its listener base. One strategy is to capture more of the 4.5 million potential listeners. The station can do this by changing formats to something more popular than alternative rock, increasing marketing, promotions, and other awareness strategies, or purchasing a competitor. In these cases, the costs would be calculated as sales, general, and administrative costs (SG&A). A project budget would be created and justified based on the overall success of the specific program. There would be no ongoing operational costs for these projects. The additional costs per additional listener would be nearly insignificant, and the additional ad revenue from reaching a broader base would (hopefully) offset that charge.

However, to add another 5 miles to its broadcast radius would require a significant additional capital investment. Fixed costs to build a new tower, hire operating personnel, secure real estate for the transmitter, etc., would be hundreds of thousands, if not millions of dollars. Once the tower was up, the per-user variable cost would be roughly equivalent to the fully or partially depreciated region at a fraction of a cent per listener. The cost model then resembles a large initial step, relatively flat for a range of listeners, then moderate-to-large steps to increase geographic reach, and therefore listener base.

2.3.2 Streaming media cost structures are low on fixed, heavy on variable

The Internet model is nearly the opposite of the digital or streaming media model. The upfront costs can be as low as $5,000, which include mid-range Intel-based server hardware, a copy of Windows.NET server software with Windows Media Server, and a connection to the Internet. This is a simple, straightforward, and cheap model. However, the per-user variable costs for digital or streaming media can be extremely high, primarily because delivering digital media over the Internet incurs a delivery charge for each and every person who requests it.

There are three elements to Internet delivery costs that correlate to the segments of the content delivery value chain. The First Mile costs are the servers, both for the servers themselves and for surrounding services to keep the servers going, such as personnel, data center space, electricity, and network connectivity gear (routers, switches, firewalls, etc.). Each server can handle a given number of simultaneous connections, as many as 4000 or as few as 40, depending on the output capacity.[5] IT departments are cautious with their server capacity and generally add a new server when the steady load uses up 40 to 50 percent of the connections available. The objective is to limit the risk that a sudden surge in users, or "flash flood," will overwhelm the servers themselves. Server load balancers spread out incoming requests over the available servers.

Server expense is analogous to that for broadcasting transmitters, but on a vastly smaller scale. Once the server availability hits a specified level, a new server is added. Much like building a new tower extends the radio station's reach to an additional 500,000 listeners, adding a new server increases the con-

---

[5] The actual number of simultaneous connections depends on the encoding bit rate, length of file, and a series of other criteria. This is discussed in more detail in Chapter 5.

current users by 40–4,000. The difference is that while increasing broadcast range can cost millions of dollars, increasing the number of available simultaneous connections is usually less than $20,000, and can be less than $10,000.

Few companies actually host all of their servers themselves. Service providers with digital media expertise handle highly specialized IT functions like media serving more effectively and efficiently than a company whose main focus is something non-IT oriented, such as producing original content or making automobiles. The two most common approaches are either (1) to outsource all hosting/serving operations, or (2) to design a hybrid model where average, daily operations are handled in-house, but service providers are engaged on an as-needed basis to increase capacity for big events or as a protection against flash crowds.

The Middle Mile costs for digital media delivery are captured in one word: bandwidth. Generally measured in megabits per second (Mbps), bandwidth costs are a function of many elements, such as the file size; distance delivered; time of day; whether it is live stream, on-demand, or download-then-play; and aggregate volume of content delivered. File size can also vary depending on the encoding rate, playback duration, and compression strategies employed. To give a rough estimate for delivery costs, prime time delivery of an Internet radio broadcast at 18 Kbps to 10,000 users can cost $0.10 to 0.20 per listener. Using peer-to-peer technologies and CDNs may get that down to $0.05 per listener or lower. To the best of the author's knowledge, no Internet radio station has reached a high enough penetration rate, and therefore enough bandwidth volume, to negotiate bandwidth costs down to sub-cent per-listener costs.

Delivering radio audio streams is much less expensive than delivering video, due to the large file size. Supplemental delivery strategies, such as multicasting, CDNs, managed delivery, or peer-to-peer technologies are essential to reduce the per-user cost of delivery, and they are discussed in greater length in Chapter 5. These strategies don't have the same effect in all situations. CDNs and peer-to-peer require an audience of some scale before they become cost-effective, generally in excess of 10,000 users or more. Managed delivery solutions can aid in delivering content that doesn't need to be used instantly, but don't work in real-time streaming or webcasting.

The Last Mile delivery costs are not as immediately tangible as the First and Middle Mile costs. These costs are associated with how a company measures usage of the content, ensures playback quality at the desktop, and collects any fees that may be associated with content usage. The costs are also associated with DRM systems to secure content, as well as the damages inflicted by theft or breaches of security. The closest analogy in the entertainment world is the Nielsen ratings system, which collects a "statistically significant" sampling in order to determine overall user behavior.

Until late 2002, executives at most media and entertainment companies believed these Last Mile costs were too high, partly because the magnitude of the costs were unknown (How do we measure usage? How much content is being stolen?) and partly because of the lingering impact of early failures in the industry (Napster, the "free" Madonna concert of 2001). Risk of theft is playing a smaller role as DRM systems mature. A rough estimate of the Last Mile costs per user ranges from $0.02 to 0.10. This estimate depends upon the size of the operation, which can include DRM, monitoring, payment reconciliation systems, and customer support. Again, service providers offer packages for these systems to either supplement or replace internal systems.

Most companies interviewed by the author indicated that they use a per-user metric when determining the costs of their Internet ventures. The deciding question is: How much will it cost to build and operate a system for our user base? From there, a consumer-oriented company can determine the per-user charge for their service or the per-impression revenue they need from advertisements. For corporations and private usage, the total system costs often erroneously consider the entire system as a fixed cost. Consequently, when the company increases or expands the usage of their system, they are not prepared for the additional per-user First, Middle, and Last Mile costs involved. These companies should take their cue from consumer companies and determine where the break-even number of customers is, not just the total system costs.

In summary, this discussion makes clear that, although traditional broadcasting is concerned with covering fixed costs, the Internet world must focus on covering variable costs. The advantage of the lower start-up costs on the Internet is that businesses can be built to serve smaller audiences, both public and private. The disadvantage is that, on the Internet, the per-user costs to scale operations have driven countless companies out of business.

2.4 Why broadcast quality is different from Internet quality

Broadcast quality is as different from Internet quality as a spotlight is from a flashlight: Both do the same thing, but to radically different degrees and for widely different purposes. Broadcast quality has matured over the past 50 years to become almost as reliable as a light switch. It is assumed by any user of a television or radio that, if the signal quality is poor, it is most probably the receiver or the cable provider that is at fault. Rarely does a consumer consider calling NBC if *The Nightly News with Tom Brokaw* is fuzzy or cuts out mid-broadcast. Instead, the television is smacked, and the cable operator's customer service lines are flooded with complaints.

On the Internet, quality responsibility is a complex mix for most consumers. The service provider is certainly the first stop, as in the television model. But what if one site works and another doesn't? The blame for poor quality quickly devolves to the site owner. If CNN.com is available and NBC.com is not, then NBC is blamed.

Quality variations as users move from page to page within a site certainly cause consternation and a wounded brand. With entertainment and media, quality is paramount. Major studios will not actively use Internet distribution until the experience for the consumer is on par with other media. Poor performance can hurt a valuable brand that has been built over time.

Corporate digital media also has quality concerns, but not to the same degree. In most instances, business uses of digital media do not need to equal television or radio quality. This is because, in a business context, users have no choice in how they consume the media. There is no comparison made in the user's mind between the viewing quality of a sales presentation and a made-for-TV movie. Instead, the important threshold for corporate digital media is "business quality access"—quality sufficient to convey the information required—so that presentation does not detract or distract from the message conveyed. For example, with a "talking head" lecture series the audio needs to come through clearly and a representation of the speaker is important, but the video portion doesn't need to show every wrinkle or blink of the speaker.

2.4.1 Start-up time

Users of digital media evaluate quality based on three parameters: start-up time, playback consistency, and playback size (for video). In a culture where consumers are conditioned for immediate gratification, patience is not a virtue but a sign of weakness. Users expect the same results from all of their digital media, whether it is playing from a CD in the disc drive or from a hosted server half a world away. Studies performed by various research groups in the late 1990s came up with the eight-second rule: If a user has to wait longer than eight seconds between when the content is requested and when it is received, the user will either hit the refresh button or move on to a more responsive site. For e-commerce, that means a lost sales opportunity. For business environments, that means a failed communication cutting down the productivity of their employees.

Start-up time should be measured as the time between when the request is made and when it is fulfilled. For small objects it may only take milliseconds. As more audio and video is used, the time stretches into seconds, minutes, or even hours. Sometimes the delay is intentional: Not everything on the Internet is designed to be delivered instantly. Video delivery services such as MovieLink use download manager clients to transfer content over a period of time ranging from 30 minutes to several hours. Although this model does not fit current customer expectations, one advantage is that bandwidth costs can be lowered by a factor of 10. There are other business problems with the download model, such as poor availability of content and consumer preferences to watch motion picture entertainment sitting on the couch with a wide-screen television and home theater surround sound. However, long start-up delays certainly factor heavily into preventing wider adoption of entertainment to the desktop.

In a business environment, start-up delay isn't much of a factor. Although users lose productivity, one effective alternative is to load training materials onto CD-ROMs and videotapes and then express mail them around the country or across the globe. Corporate users need predictable delivery, not instantaneous delivery. If the video is delivered by 9 a.m. Tuesday morning, and the user knows that is the delivery time, then it can take whatever time necessary to be delivered as long as it arrives by the scheduled time. The start-up latency would then be calculated from how long after 9 a.m. the user had to wait for their delivery to arrive.

2.4.2 Playback consistency

Playback consistency refers to the steadiness at which the digital or streaming media plays out after it has been initiated. Nothing starts phones ringing off the hook at call centers like interruptions, skips, frozen frames, dropped video, or other inconsistent playback. Consistency is the key. Users set their expectation of what playback should be during the first 10–15 seconds of an audio or video track. If the experience is poor, the user will not continue with the playback. If the quality is acceptable during the initial period, that quality becomes the base level against which the rest of the media experience is judged. Variations from that base cause the user or consumer to believe that there is a problem.

As in start-up time, the consumer audience is much more demanding than their business user counterparts. Whether or not a fee is involved, consumers judge playback consistency against other entertainment media. Television shows do not stop and start. Audio quality may vary from one compact disc to another, but each compact disc has the same audio quality from beginning to end.

2.4.3 Playback size (for video)

Size does matter, particularly during video playback. IP-delivered video the size of a postage stamp is no longer considered acceptable in most situations, especially not for broadband consumers or corporate users. At the same time, the video does not need to cover a full 17-inch screen. Consumers want a choice of either a higher bit rate, and therefore larger format video, or a lower bit rate and smaller format video. Advances in compression technologies from Microsoft, RealNetworks, Apple, and the MPEG-LA Group allow VCR-quality playback in a near full-screen size of 300 Kbps.

Contrary to the initial expectation, business users didn't need a screen size similar to consumers, as corporate streaming and digital media is just as effective—if not more so—in a smaller format. The reason for the smaller format is that video in a business setting is generally one part of a larger application. Video and audio add value to the overall application, but are not the primary value themselves. That is not true for most consumer uses of digital and streaming media, where the value is inherent to the content itself. Therefore, in playback size, consumers demand to see what they are paying for, either through direct fees or through viewing the neighboring advertisements. In a business environment, audio and video help convey the message, but they are not the entire message, so the playback size can be small and still be effective.

2.5 Typical quality measurements for streaming and digital media

Content owners need to know who is watching their movies and listening to their audio streams, regardless of whether they are addressing a consumer or user audience. In the consumer world, audience monitoring and measurement is critical to charging advertising fees. Without size and demographic information, the cost per impression quickly becomes miniscule, which is why revenue from Internet banner and pop-ads dropped through the floor during the tech wreck of 2001 and 2002. About 2,000 ads were served during June 2001, but there was only a 0.02 percent click-through rate that took the viewer to the ad sponsor. Why so low? It is impossible to tell. Perhaps the ad was not visible or vibrant enough to capture the consumer's attention. More likely, the ad was shown to any random person associated with the site instead of potential customers of the advertiser.

2.5.1 Why Nielsen and Arbitron have had trouble measuring a digital media audience

Audience monitoring and measurement for broadcast entertainment has been handed over to the Nielsen rating system and Arbitron. Using a specific statistical methodology that spreads measuring devices among a "representative population" of television viewers, these companies then collect, standardize, and aggregate the data, so that viewer's behavior is only represented to content providers and advertisers in aggregate. It is an imperfect yet perfectly acceptable solution, particularly when there is no "feedback loop" between a television set or radio receiver and the broadcaster to tell the content provider what each user is doing.

With IP-based systems, there is a feedback loop. The TCP/IP protocols require a handshake between requester and receiver for each connection made. There is a unique IP address for every computer, network element, or server in the world. Authorization and authentication systems commonly use IP addresses and username/password registered users to control access to content. Combining these technologies, it is possible to determine what every user is doing at any given time on the Internet.

The problem with this type of monitoring is twofold: privacy and volume. Most nations have consumer privacy acts that prevent companies from manipulating user data in a way that would target an individual user for a specific product or service. In western nations, there is constant tension between personal privacy and public responsibility. Some people express it like this: My right to swing my fist ends when it hits your face. The ability to identify any individual's actions on the Internet raises the hackles of personal privacy advocates. Certainly the attacks of 9/11 and other terrorism threats have imposed limitations on individual privacy, because the threat of a fist hitting someone's face feels real and present. In addition, given the differences in laws between different nations and the interconnectedness of the Internet, anti-pornography laws and distribution of other illegal content poses a legal quandary. Considering these complicated issues, the pendulum will continue to swing from side to side for some time.

The second half of the problem is the sheer volume of information that is moved around the Internet. The average Web page takes 14–20 individual transactions to transfer to an end-user's machine. The latest count of Web pages in the world was around 3 trillion. Tracking all those transfers would lead to a tremendous amount of data collected at every second of every day. Which data are the most important? How do you cut through the noise to find the relevant information?

Most digital and streaming media content providers are satisfied with information that is very basic: the number of unique visitors, the number of content downloads, and the number of simultaneous connections. While important for capacity and operations planning by the IT departments and service providers, these numbers quickly lose their relevance in a business context. Advertisers pay to target market segments with particular demographic or behavioral criteria, not to reach 2 million faceless visitors per month.

The current trend in Web site viewers is to create "communities of interest," in which individuals agree to give up a little anonymity in return for privileged access or priority service. Individual sites can then begin to understand the geographic, demographic, and behavioral makeup of their constituencies.

The sampling services of Nielsen and Arbitron are nearly ineffective in the Internet environment. Most communities of interest are too small to register as a statistically significant target group. For those groups that are large enough, the geographic spread makes targeting that group through alternative forms of media difficult if not impossible. In the end, the value of a company like Nielsen and Arbitron will be to aggregate the mass of data and extract meaningful user groups, cross-tab correlations, and other business-relevant information. Thus far, privacy and volume have thwarted most of these efforts. Again, there is a distinct difference between monitoring and measuring the consumer-oriented audience and the business environment as legal systems are still working out what is "private" within a corporate network.

Aside from legal/illegal activities, many enterprises require some sort of user monitoring and measurement to prove regulatory compliance to the relevant regulatory board, such as the Occupational Health and Safety Administration (OSHA) or the Securities and Exchange Commission (SEC). Digital and streaming media can be used for training and education in order to provide employee safety training, public disclosure of financial announcements, and other actions that comply with the particular regulatory board. Audience monitoring and management tools become essential for these applications.

Just as the privacy issue is not as important, neither is the volume problem at present. Validation must occur for perhaps hundreds or maybe thousands of employees. Rarely does the volume reach the level of even a "small" mass consumer audience of a few hundred thousand.

2.6 Content security: digital media means a user can record an exact copy

This section on technical background concerns content security. Unlike other mediums, digital audio and video content enables near-perfect duplication at a low cost. Therefore, copies of media are virtually the same as the original. Also, the original does not degrade over time or from the duplication process, so a single original can be the source for as many copies as a user wishes to make. This is why the profit margins of Microsoft and other software companies are 25–75 percent.

This is also why owners of digital content are paranoid about theft: If the copy is as good as the original, why should someone purchase the original? Below are four strategies currently employed to secure content.

2.6.1 Digital rights management and content encryption

Encryption scrambles the piece of content itself, so that it cannot be viewed without the decryption key. Encryption is separate from encoding: It puts the file in a virtual safe, while encoding formats the file for a particular media platform. Many DRM solutions use asynchronous systems, i.e., the key is not tied to the safe but kept somewhere else on the Internet. The user requests and receives the file but needs to perform a separate transaction in order to secure the appropriate decryption key. The danger with this type of delivery is that smart thieves crack open the safe and start spreading the file in an unencrypted format. Anarchist hackers fighting for "free information everywhere" believe it their mission in life to crack every safe and share the contents. Once a piece of content starts spreading unencrypted, the value is lost to the content owner.

DRM is undergoing a rapid evolution. As each new security system is hacked, a stronger and better one is built to replace it. Microsoft, for example, is developing a counterintuitive form of DRM for music files. This includes placing the key on the physical medium itself, so that a CD cannot be played unless the consumer has the physical CD. If the file is copied to a computer or another disc and is no longer on the same physical CD as the key, it becomes permanently encrypted. Ultimately, this system, too, will be broken, and another one will take its place. The challenge is that each successive generation of solutions gets progressively more expensive. It is conceivable that we may end up with an unbreakable system that costs far too much to use on a widespread basis.

2.6.2 Walled gardens

Walled garden content security places a virtual barrier around a content set, which requires a user to purchase access with an authorization/authentication system. The *Wall Street Journal*, for example, has a public facing site, freely available to anyone. It also has a "premium content" site for which individuals pay a monthly or annual fee. Almost every type of content has a walled garden option.

The value of walled gardens is intricately tied to longevity. Once inside, a permitted user can download, copy, and distribute whatever content he or she would like. The value for the content owner must be based on this assumption. The content gains value not because it can't be stolen, but because the owner refreshes the content regularly and rapidly. The *Wall Street Journal* has new content every morning. CNN's video content appears as stories develop. Adult and religious walled garden sites constantly add new audio streams, video clips, or images to entice return viewers and continued subscribers.

2.6.3 The "cheap and easy access" security strategy

Apple Computer's phenomenal success with iTunes Music Service proves there is another option for content security: To prevent something from being stolen, make it available at a price that is less than the cost to steal it. The majority of consumers in the world are honest people. Give them what they want, at a price they can afford, and in an easily consumable manner, and they will purchase it rather than steal it.

This simple system is not effective, though, when consumers have already been conditioned in one direction, for example, free music. It is also not effective for content whose value is derived from scarcity, which is why Disney only re-releases its animated classics every seven years: A new generation can enjoy it, and in the intervening years, an artificial scarcity drives up the value of the content. At some point, the recording industry will have to write off the value of all music that has already been lost to file sharing and piracy. That music is out on the Internet, and regardless of how many individuals or file-sharing services are closed down, there will always be alternatives sprouting up. Consumers are also conditioned to get music for free. Until such time as it is either cheap and easy to purchase any song or album at any time the consumer wishes, or content security is affordable and secure enough to prevent new music from being copied and spread via the Internet, music distribution over the Internet will continue unabated.

2.6.4 PC client content/download managers

A relatively new approach to content security is to require consumers or users to install a small content or download management client on their PC. This application is connected to a dedicated service provided by the content owner or a content aggregator, who is the wholesale intermediary between a set of content owners and end users. Download managers can facilitate content distribution by using peer-to-peer or throttling strategies to move the content to the consumer's machine. More important, they can act as the DRM enforcement engine and audience monitoring and management application as well as other functions. The client can then enforce content security, whether or not the PC is connected to the Internet.

The disadvantage of this approach is that, like any piece of software, download managers can be hacked. With enough diligence or a smart enough cyber thief, even the most secure download manager can be broken.

2.7 Case studies

2.7.1 palmOne

palmOne, Inc. makes products used by customers around the world. To further strengthen relationships with its customers while improving its bottom line, palmOne turned to the Kontiki Delivery Management System (DMS). Kontiki (www.kontiki.com) gives palmOne better customer support at lower cost by automating the delivery of video-based set-up guides for its products. These video guides give customers easy-to-follow demonstrations covering common support inquiries. They are available around the clock around the world, which represents a step up in service and a step down in cost.

For makers of handheld computing devices, the most necessary feature is ease of use. palmOne broke through in this marketplace in the 1990s with a combined hardware-software solution with an intuitive interface that revolutionized the market for personal digital assistants (PDAs). Competition and technology improvements have driven the price of the PDAs down while adding more features. This attracted countless new customers who were new to the world of PDAs and often technophobic. In turn, this drove up call volumes to palmOne's support center. Calls were often longer and hence more expensive. As competitive pressure and technological breakthroughs drove down the price of palmOne products, these calls represented an ever-increasing drain on the bottom line. palmOne considered and rejected remedies such as phone trees because of low customer satisfaction with such methods.

For palmOne, many customer calls focused on how to set up and perform a HotSync operation that transfers information between the PDA and a desktop computer. palmOne had previously implemented set-up and support guides on its Web site to help users with the set-up process, but the company felt they were still getting too many support calls on this and other basic questions. palmOne needed to add a new dimension to its customer support, so that buyers with questions could really see and understand basic processes without needing to talk directly with a customer support representative. palmOne wanted to be able to deliver this information without requiring significant upgrades to its Web site and networking infrastructure.

palmOne has always emphasized value and simplicity in its products, and knows its customers expect the same in their communications with the company. For this reason, they embraced digital video as a customer communications medium, and chose the Kontiki DMS as the solution for managing and delivering its support videos to customers. The system provided palmOne with easy-to-use application tools for the publishing and management of support videos and also helped palmOne seamlessly integrate the videos into its customer support Web site. The DMS also made it easy for palmOne to reach large customer audiences by tapping computers throughout the palmOne Network to deliver video content faster without expensive network upgrades.

palmOne simply added the video delivery features to its existing set-up and support guides, which offered customers an additional easy-to-follow way to receive answers to their important support questions. The Kontiki delivery grid then delivered these digital videos to palmOne's customers. Customers received these full-motion videos by simply installing the Kontiki delivery manager—easy-to-use, lightweight Windows software, which enabled efficient, secure delivery of digital video to users' desktops. The delivery manager lets users view all types of digital media and documents. This content is easily integrated into existing Web sites, and users just click on links to have content automatically downloaded to their machines.

This digital media system also provides palmOne with custom response bars, which appear below videos playing on the user's desktop. Using the response bars and simple HTML programming, palmOne can lead users toward other materials that further reduce the need for telephone support. The response bars also introduce customers to new palmOne products and services, thus driving revenue. The success of the initial customer support videos has led palmOne to expand its approach to include videos on how to configure and use such advanced features as WiFi, Bluetooth, and more.

The response from customers has been increased satisfaction and fewer "live" calls to support staff. In a survey of more than 900 palmOne users, two-thirds of the respondents cited two features as important to them in receiving video: a high-quality, full-screen picture and the ability to watch offline and stop or pause the video. Kontiki provides palmOne with both these features, which many other video delivery systems don't offer. More than one-third of survey respondents said the video answered their questions, thus avoiding the need for personal help by customer support staff. The benefit of this system alone is saving palmOne an estimated $370,000 per year in customer service costs. User satisfaction is also very high for delivered video support. The majority of users prefer video demonstrations over phone, e-mail, or an online knowledge-based search.

This success led palmOne to expand its use of digital media to another key part of its business—delivering new software programs and updates to the desktops of palmOne owners for installation into their products. More than 600,000 such downloads, frequently topping 20 MB each, are delivered every year. Kontiki lowers palmOne's costs for these downloads by making the most efficient use of existing bandwidth, which allows palmOne to cancel an expensive contract for additional peak-usage bandwidth. Adding it up, palmOne saves nearly two times its investment in Kontiki every year. That's why palmOne is planning additional uses for employing digital video at different points in the product life cycle for demonstrations, reseller training, and media briefings.

2.7.2 Ernst & Young

Ernst & Young, one of the world's largest professional services firms, is committed to restoring the public's trust in professional service firms and in the quality of financial reporting. In more than 140 countries its employees face challenges internally as well as externally as they work with colleagues to understand the implications of recent legislation. They also face challenges as they work with clients to ensure that corporate governance and adherence to strict ethical standards form the cornerstone of their businesses.

Today, a business video-on-demand solution is allowing Ernst & Young to cost-effectively deliver high-quality video communications to all employees. Examples of these types of communications include:

- Effectively communicating critical directives in corporate governance, regulations, and strategic practices from the very top of the organization to every employee

- Ensuring that members of globally distributed practice groups can stay on the same page and more effectively complete their jobs with targeted communications
- Providing effective education of new hires, including recent college graduates, so that they meet the high standards of the firm
- Fostering organizational knowledge and adherence to evolving best practices as determined by leaders within each business unit or industry group
- Deploying effective "high-touch" communications and training to all employees without requiring expensive upgrades to the existing network infrastructure

The Sarbanes-Oxley Act (SOA), passed in mid-2002, was meant to address the crisis in corporate confidence. SEC regulations are now beginning to spell out more precisely what SOA will mean to companies. But one thing is clear: Businesses must be more transparent, more accountable, and pay more attention to what is happening internally if trust is to be restored. This includes managing intangibles such as the corporate culture and organizational ethics.

Ernst & Young believes a "principles-based approach" to corporate governance requires that key changes in policies and procedures be thoroughly defined by those at the top and communicated quickly and effectively to the ranks. How should they communicate effectively with impact and power? To John McCreadie, chief information officer (CIO) of Ernst & Young, the answer was obvious—business video. As John McCreadie commented: "We believe that by using business video-on-demand for corporate communications and training, we can maximize the return on our greatest asset, our employees." He asked the Ernst & Young IT department to investigate solutions that would allow him to utilize business video for globally distributed communications and training.

Searching for a solution

Ernst & Young had a number of technical "must haves" when it began searching for a solution. They felt the solution needed to:

- Provide sufficient functionality and flexibility to universally reach all employees in a timely manner through on-demand and "push" video broadcasting
- Enable "narrowcast" communications that are targeted and secure so that geographically dispersed practice groups could efficiently communicate

- Enable flexible video delivery options, including push (automatically sending video to selected recipients), pull (fulfilling user on-demand requests for video), subscription (periodic video delivery), and e-mail
- Deliver video globally without requiring expensive network upgrades or impacting country network capacities
- Support a highly mobile workforce where employees often move between offices or need to access information from locations outside of the corporate network
- Provide the capability to protect sensitive corporate information by leveraging DRM technology and existing directory services

The solution

Kontiki is providing Ernst & Young with a complete end-to-end solution for business video-on-demand with network-friendly delivery for all employees worldwide. The solution includes:

1. Kontiki Delivery Management System 3.0: The DMS 3.0 is a software suite that allows Ernst & Young to publish, protect, deliver, and measure video and other rich media. This enables video communications and training for all Ernst & Young employees worldwide. It also includes grid delivery technology, which enables secure and centrally managed delivery of video while greatly minimizing the amount of bandwidth and hardware required for full-screen, high-quality video communications.
2. System integration: Using XML Web Services, Kontiki is seamlessly integrated with Ernst & Young's enterprise-wide list management technology—the Global List Management System (GLMS)—to allow flexible narrowcast delivery of video to targeted groups as well as broadcast communications to the entire workforce.
3. Business media services: Kontiki worked together with Ernst & Young to identify opportunities that easily and cost-effectively created video in-house using standard software tools and inexpensive digital video cameras. For example, Kontiki helped Ernst & Young set up several "self-service" video production studios for less than $10,000 each.

How has the system worked so far? The deployment has been completed to over 106,000 desktops/laptops worldwide with high-quality video communications and training successfully delivered to achieve the stated business goals.

CHAPTER 3

The Four Keys to a Profitable Streaming or Digital Media Business

3.1 Given these technology issues, what should you focus on when building your digital media business?

Given the technology issues of Chapter 2, what are the critical components for building a profitable digital media strategy for a consumer-based service or an internal user group? This chapter builds on the previous technologies overview to provide an understanding of the following digital media businesses or services.

- The four key principles of a stable digital media strategy: scalability, security, intelligence, and quality
- How to distinguish between the relevant and the irrelevant choices that a digital media unit must make around these principles based on the focus of your business
- The potential results of trade-offs within each principle, and lessons learned from past failures and successes
- How to balance the trade-offs between the four key principles to build a profitable and/or cost-effective business model for your digital media products or services

Keep in mind that this book is a "how to" for building a solid business model around digital media. It is not a technical manual on installing digital media infrastructure, deploying routers, encoding videos, or other activities. This chapter, and the rest of the book, will include technology only where absolutely necessary for understanding the business decisions that need to be made.

3.2 Four key principles of a stable digital media strategy: scalability, security, intelligence, and quality

As with any business tasked with distributing content via digital media or otherwise, the questions you must always answer in order to be successful have to do with the reach, protection, quality, and content consumption by your end users. Companies tasked with implementing any form of digital media strategy must have a clear, concise idea of whom they are targeting and what experience they want the end user to have. Keep in mind that the power of the Internet can be used to your advantage but, as with any distribution medium, at a cost to you and your organization. To be successful, there must be a logical business strategy from the beginning in order to understand how to get a return on your investment. Many companies whose primary business is not content related are realizing that the use of digital media technology and applications enhances their current business, and it is the enhancement to their core product, not content, that generates revenue. With the constant emergence of new technology and the continual change of the digital landscape, deciding how to create a digital media business can be quite complicated. It seems as if everyone has a different answer or opinion as to what technology is the best. However, if you understand the business, impact on licensing, security, distribution, and quality, you can quickly build a successful digital media business with long-term success, no matter how technology evolves. Remember that the best or newest technology is not what is important to your strategy. The most important thing to realize is that the technology you want to utilize is the kind that is scalable, widely adopted, easy to measure, and has a direct impact on the way you do business. Technology means nothing unless it moves your business forward. You don't want to concentrate all your time and efforts on technology. The technology you use is only the means to the end, and the best technology in the world will not help a poorly conceived digital media business initiative.

3.3 Scalability: a scalable delivery strategy can cut delivery costs over traditional broadcast

As shown in Chapter 2, the number of people accessing digital media content directly impacts the cost to build and operate the business unit or service. In the early days of the Internet, many companies forgot to manage costs of distributing their content in digital form. Both content companies and those companies who were acting as the service conduits for distribution of content quickly learned the hard way. They gave content away to as many people as possible to grab the biggest market share, yet showed no profit or sustainable business model. Companies who were in the content delivery business (CDN), such as iBeam Broadcasting, quickly disappeared when their customers could no longer afford to deliver free content to everyone all of the time. Companies purchasing these services realized what the true cost of producing, managing, and distributing their content was and quickly realized the need for a targeted, focused content strategy rather than trying to just reach everyone.

Those companies not in the service business, who were using streaming and digital media as a means of communication or market awareness, didn't realize the costs associated with trying to reach a global audience. Many companies simply gave away free content with scant advertisement-supported models or any type of pay-per-view or pay-per-subscription alternatives. Hence, companies spent millions of dollars giving away content digitally simply to attract customers to their Web site, because they figured the advertisers would eventually pay to reach those customers. MTV.com, which used to produce live webcasts on a daily basis for free on the Internet to anyone who wanted to watch them, realized a few years later that the cost to produce this content far outweighed any money they received in return for advertising. When the bottom fell out of Web advertising in 2000, many content companies were stuck with great content, but no means to cover their distribution costs. So much emphasis was placed on simply grabbing market share and viewers, that companies never stopped to consider the true cost to reach users.

The scalability of one's content and its distribution reach are the largest factors that affect the cost of deploying digital media. One of the biggest advantages of using streaming and digital media technologies is the ability to reach users without geographical boundaries. However, unlike traditional models of distribution, like terrestrial radio where adding listeners has no impact on your distribution costs, digital media distribution via the Internet is the exact opposite. The more users that access, download, stream, and consume your content, the more you pay for distribution, security, and licensing.

When deploying digital media content, your first task should be to figure out who your average end user is. For an enterprise corporation streaming content to its remote offices, this answer could be fairly easy to estimate. However, if you're doing external streaming to consumers, shareholders, or employees outside the office, knowing how many users you will get, how long each user will listen or watch your content, and at what speed they view it can be a guessing game if not done right. Most digital media content is consumed on-demand, as opposed to live content. For on-demand distribution, you primarily pay for the amount of bandwidth that is distributed over a certain period of time. That distribution cost is dependent on the amount of users accessing your content and the reach. At first it may be hard to figure out the exact numbers. Many companies start off by experimenting with the types of content people consume most and in what volume. After a short period of time, you'll quickly be able to see the geographical location of your users and the average length of time they're spending watching or downloading your content. You'll also be able to see the speed at which they are accessing it, broadband versus narrowband, which will allow you to know exactly what you'll have to pay for your distribution costs. Chapter 5 covers how to estimate your audience's media consumption based on file size and length of content.

While we spoke of the radio model for distributing content versus the cost for Internet distribution, streaming and digital media over traditional broadcasts such as TV and DVD *can* greatly cut delivery costs and give you more of focused, global, and near real-time reach. Delivering media digitally gives you the opportunity to capture end-user information, which includes viewing habits and other demographics that can't be acquired via traditional broadcast means. The cost to acquire one targeted customer via the Internet is a fraction of the cost to acquire them via traditional means of print or broadcast. For the past few years, the use of digital media by many companies had been limited strictly to sending out digital content via DVDs, which would be mailed out to users wanting more information. The cost to produce, duplicate, and mail that form of media far outweighs the cost to deliver it via the Internet. This instantly gratifies the end user who is able to receive the content when they want it, how they want it, and from where they want it.

3.4 Security: digital rights management (DRM) security technologies make streaming and digital media safe and sound

Digital rights management (DRM) security technology keeps streaming and digital media content safe and sound. DRM is probably one of the hottest topics. It is continually talked about in the press and by industry experts simply because it helps to add new business models in the area of digital media. For the first time, security technology allows content creators the ability to charge for their content and actually have a sustainable business model so they can afford to produce and distribute their content on the Internet. The most important thing to remember about DRM is the broad view and scope of rights management technology. Although we hear of DRM technology associated primarily with streaming, it truly is a technology that is utilized in all forms of digital media. Any type of digital media that lets you give a user rights to specific content and perform some sort of transaction—subscription, pay-per-use, or even just authentication—is the building block for potential new business models on the Web.

The most intriguing aspect about DRM is the fact that companies have begun to understand that rights management is more about opportunity in new business models, as opposed to trying to protect the business of old ones. In the music industry, for instance, record labels have realized that people may not want to purchase an entire CD and would rather pay for just one single. While some companies, such as N2K, were doing digital download services as early as 1998, the technology that existed at the time prevented N2K's success as users were not yet ready to purchase music in a digital form. Because technology has evolved, we have seen such services as Apple's iTunes become a huge success in terms of consuming digital media on a mainstream scale. As more households become connected to the Internet, habits for consuming digital media literally change overnight in more areas than just music. A consumer may not want to purchase an annual subscription to a magazine, but may be interested in downloading just one or two of its articles. Today's DRM technology makes that possible. Digital media no longer takes away from a company's traditional brick and mortar business, but rather enhances or adds to its current revenue model.

DRM also applies to corporations that don't sell content as part of their primary source of revenue. Many corporations rely on DRM to protect information that is accompanied with other products and services they sell, which allows them to add features to their primary product. We have already seen DRM technology used extensively in document management systems such as PDFs and even Word documents. DRM technology goes way beyond security for streaming media-specific content. It is a wide-reaching scope of technology that enables users to decide who, when, what, and in what form content is accessed.

3.5 Intelligence: getting accurate, reliable, usable usage and audience intelligence

It is crucial to have accurate and reliable intelligence on the consumption usage of your audiences to build a successful digital media business. Unlike years ago, technology exists today that enables you to track and measure in detail the usage habits of your consumers. Web site cookies, registration engines, media player preferences, and transaction pieces allow you to know who's watching what and for how long. Because you have to create a budget to produce, manage, and distribute your content, knowing the viewing or listening habits of your end users is crucial in developing a realistic profit and loss. These costs are all derived from the amount of users that consume your content and the length and volume in which they consume it.

There are a few ways to track the viewing habits of your end users that will help in the success of your digital media project. One cannot ever underestimate the importance of constantly measuring the success of your business with these numbers. One of the easiest ways to do this is to make sure that you receive detailed reporting from your service provider or the CDN that is delivering your content. No matter what technology is used, all streaming media software used on the servers to distribute your content comes with the ability to save "logs" that record what is taking place. Your service provider then puts these logs into an easy-to-read format or software application so you can understand what is taking place with your media. Although reporting varies from each service provider, there is a basic set of details you should be interested in.

- Total megabytes transferred
- Views by clip, visitor, and time period
- Player and version type
- Average view time duration

- Maximum number of simultaneous users (peak audience size), with date, time, and average viewers
- Unique viewers
- Most frequent visitors
- Storage utilization per client at time of billing and max peak used in a month
- Total number of user sessions
- Maximum number of simultaneous users per clip
- File popularity (the amount of file accesses over a specific period)
- Successful requests, failed requests, and number of requests that didn't transfer completely

Additionally, when distributing your content, you can require users to register via your Web site to be able to access the content. User-required registration enables you to better track who's watching and their preferences. More important, it allows you to have detailed information on those users and gives you a way to reach out to them for feedback, additional sales pitches, and timely communication. Unlike years ago, user-based registration is now considered standard for nearly all Web sites distributing content, and end users, for the most part, don't mind registering.

I'm often asked by corporations who have detailed reporting how they gauge success based on their report numbers. Depending on the business, there are a few ways to do this. To begin with, ask: Is it costing you more to produce and deliver your content than the revenue you are receiving in return? For companies not selling content the question should be: Are you getting the reach, exposure, and number of viewers you expected for your money? Whether you spend $1,000 or $10,000 on a digital media project, no investment is worth the money if you are not prepared to judge its success. Having a defined set of parameters that allows you to see your return on investment (ROI) is essential. You should also judge the metrics based on the quality of the message you delivered: Was it clear, concise, and delivered in the format you wanted?

You should also talk to other companies in your industry to compare notes and see how they are utilizing digital media and how they measure their success. There are many case studies by vendors that showcase their clients' adoption of technology and the ways their success was measured. In addition, industry metrics companies such as Keynote and Arbitron give industry demographics and end-user habits for consuming media on the Web, which you may find helpful.

To help illustrate this point, the latest numbers from a report released in 2004 by the Aberdeen Group in conjunction with visitors of the www.streamingmedia.com Web site have been provided in Appendix A. These numbers showcase what type of media users are consuming, what their preferences are, and what applications they are using. This report proves that *now* is the time to aggressively engage, or re-engage, in the use of streaming and digital media in business and personal applications for cost savings, revenue opportunities, and customer interaction.

The reader has heard this claim before, but now there is proof that the numbers are real. The report from the Aberdeen Group is a statistically valid benchmark study that points the way to streaming and digital media success. It proves that:

1. A mature, experienced user base now exists. Enterprises and content providers can now deploy streaming and digital media and be confident that internal employees and external customers can have a solid experience with media in a variety of contexts.
2. Firms who have deployed streaming applications in some business areas (e.g., distance learning, webcasting) should look to other applications (e.g., product launches, executive communications) that build on those successes.
3. Company executives, IT professionals, and content providers who are dabbling in media usage should move toward expanding their deployments.

This report shows that users are actively engaging the streaming and digital media applications available to them. The Executive Summary in Appendix A highlights the key findings from this report in relation to business applications and use, personal applications and use, and overall media usage.

In addition to having accurate intelligence on user habits, you must present your content intelligently. As a general rule, most audio and video clips should be about five minutes in length and segmented into chapters. Longer than five minutes should be the rare exception on the Web. For example, instead of putting an entire 30-minute keynote lecture on the Web as streaming audio or video, put up text files with a transcript. If possible, employ an editor to edit the transcript into something that is more readable than most lectures. Next, supplement the text with a few photos of the speaker and the audience as well as high-quality versions of any visuals. Finally, you can communicate the speaker's personality and the spirit of the event by linking to clips of the most exciting sound bites. Your average user will not sit through a 30-minute lecture when all they want are its high points. In the case of a live webcast, user viewership tends to be longer. The nature of the delivered content is perceived to be more important because it is live, so viewers will watch for a longer period of time.

To preserve the feeling of user control with on-demand content, even when presenting multimedia, edit longer presentations into short chapters that can be chosen from a menu. For example, when converting a television news program to the Web, don't make it into a single, 60-minute streaming video that can't be controlled by the user. Instead, break the program into one segment for each news story. Then prepare a standard Web page that lists the stories with a short summary and a single thumbnail photo from the most visual ones. Allow users to link to individual stories from this page. If you are creative in how you present your content and treat your users like they are intelligent, your chances of success will instantly increase.

3.6 Quality: assuring media fidelity and quality when delivering content over the Internet

No matter what business vertical you are in, the quality of the content you are delivering is one of the factors that will determine your success in online digital media. The saying "garbage in, garbage out" also applies to the Internet. End users always expect a certain level of quality, and your business plan must reflect this. However, keep in mind that the Internet is a different distribution medium than traditional broadcast. Years ago many users expected TV quality video on their computer, but today's reality is that end users consuming digital media realize that they are giving up some quality for ease of use and instant access. Technology has come full circle and a low bit rate streaming audio file sounds just as good as FM quality audio over the radio. Additionally, distribution models—such as P2P or downloads where the file is completely downloaded to the user's computer before playback—allow for greater quality, as evidenced when Apple did the big Star Wars movie trailer download.

Some content broadcasts better than others over the Internet, but all content has to have a certain level of audio and video quality for users to accept the delivered information (see Chapter 5). Also, the quality of the actual delivery is important. You may have a well-produced video file, but if the distribution medium delivering it is of poor quality or slow, that content may not make it to the end user. So, assuring quality is really twofold, both to the actual source content and in the delivery of that content.

3.7 Case studies

3.7.1 JP Morgan/Chase

Since the introduction of streaming media technology, many corporations have seen the potential for the applications that harness the power of this technology. One such company is JPMorgan Chase. It has been successful in leveraging this technology to reduce cost, improve communications, and market its services.

Chase, which merged with JPMorgan in December 2000, started implementing and experimenting with streaming media technology back in 1998 when a pilot program was launched to extend the reach and effectiveness of the daily morning international research conference calls. Streaming technology was originally implemented into audio-only content as an enhancement to traditional telephone conferencing, not as a replacement. Over time, however, it became clear that offering on-demand replays of meetings or events via the intranet was not only more convenient than dialing a replay number by phone, but could also save a substantial amount of money by eliminating conference service storage costs. Audio quality was superior as well. A study was commissioned to compare the leading streaming media technologies and the ability of the Chase global infrastructure to handle the traffic reliably without negatively impacting existing systems. Initially, satellite servers were installed in the main offices of the headquarters, which limited the audience to those locations. Over the next several years, more servers, or proxies, were installed, thereby increasing the coverage area.

Two-thirds of the streaming done at JPMorgan Chase is for internal communications and training and is delivered on demand as opposed to live, although they are seeing the amount of live broadcasts grow every quarter. The majority of the content produced and delivered is done using in-house resources and personnel. JPMorgan Chase has a dedicated team in the broadcast services division that is focused on streaming media. They use high-end miniDV camcorders and record to DVCAM as well as doing their own audio and video mixing and processing in order to guarantee the quality of the finished production. If the event is live, they capture digitally to a computer and back up to DVCAM. This allows the fastest turnaround if no editing is required. If editing is required, they capture from the DVCAM to either a Mac or PC system and edit the content using standard NLE software. Once content is ready for serving, it is uploaded to internal streaming servers for distribution. Although most of the content produced and delivered is done internally, the team does use external CDNs for large-scale events and content delivered via the Internet. The JPMorgan Chase core streaming platform is primarily RealNetworks, although Windows Media is also used and is found on all of the desktops.

JPMorgan Chase has built a winning formula for streamlining the flow of information internally within the company. "The overall strategy for internal communications focuses on bringing a company with offices all around the world into a smaller environment, so people feel connected, which makes the sharing of information much easier," says David Nolan, Senior Vice President of Branding & Advertising. Clearly, JPMorgan Chase has been successful incorporating streaming media technology into its business and continues to develop new ways to integrate its benefits in the corporate environment.

3.7.2 Unisys

Unisys is a worldwide information technology services and solutions company that combines expertise in systems integration, outsourcing, infrastructure, server technology, and consulting. With operations in over 100 countries, Unisys has over 37,000 employees and generates nearly $6 billion in annual sales. Its goal is to implement a cost-effective and reliable method of communicating corporate, product, and training information to employees located in more than 100 countries. Once this goal was met, Unisys needed to expand the system to provide a professional and interactive method of communicating externally with customers, investors, and partners over the Internet.

Traditionally, Unisys relied heavily on a satellite communication system that was incapable of reaching all of their offices and didn't support communications to the general public. Although the network could have been expanded, Unisys considered this alternative cost-prohibitive. Instead, they sought a more cost-effective solution that could be used to reach every office and meet a growing need to communicate to customers, investors, and partners over the Internet. After briefly using an outsourced, hosted solution, Unisys initiated a technology review to bring the solution in-house. After evaluating several technology vendors, Unisys selected Accordent's (www.accordent.com) PresenterPRO Enterprise Edition as their in-house Web presentation solution. See Figure 3.1 for an example of a typical Unisys live webcast interface.

Unisys selected PresenterPRO because this program supported its live and on-demand webcasts; could work both internally, behind the firewall, and for external webcasts; and was able to work on the existing infrastructure. According to Angela Haynes, Special Projects/Business Development, Pre-

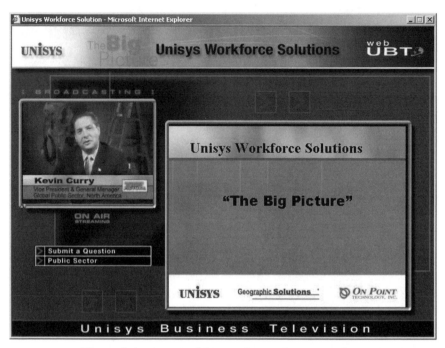

Figure 3.1: *A typical Unisys live webcast interface.*

senterPRO enabled Unisys "to easily customize skins for every business unit and for every presentation." Unisys has been using this digital media system for over a year and, during that time, it has expanded its use of webcasting far beyond the initial expectations. Unisys currently webcasts every presentation produced by Unisys Business Television and, over the course of the year, has webcast more than 100 internal and external presentations. "When we first implemented the solution, I don't think that we planned to video stream every single presentation," said Angela Haynes, "but from day one, we did every single broadcast with the software. We jumped in big and a year later, the solution has way exceeded our expectations." Additionally, this digital media solution has provided Unisys with a flexible means that customizes the presentations based upon their intended audience, reduces their costs and time associated with creating content, and gives them flexible distribution options other than just satellite. "Sending out video on the Internet is one thing, but sending out a message that works is another thing. There are two components to a webcast, one is the video and the other is the graphic and supporting material . . . and Accordent allowed us to make it perfect . . . in a way that it will impact people," stated Steve Fanelli, Vice President, Creative Media Services.

CHAPTER 4

It's Not Child's Play: Learning from the Pitfalls of the Past Three Years

4.1 In the Internet land grab and rush for revenue, early companies forgot to manage the costs for streaming and digital delivery

As streaming media technology started to become popular in the late 1990s, many companies focused heavily on either the technology or the content side of the equation. They neglected the business surrounding their content and mistakenly paid little attention to the costs associated with creating, securing, and distributing their content. They also got so caught up in the marketing hype of needing to advertise that they were using the newest technology and they sacrificed user adoption and accessibility. Sidetracked by technology, companies ignored the cost associated with licensing or purchasing new products and services.

Many companies failed as a consequence of not understanding all of the components that go into a digital media strategy and the cost to purchase or use those components. This chapter details what you need to be aware of when looking at the different types of technology available on the market and the mistakes previously made by other companies. No technology is worth anything unless it has a proven value on how it will move your business forward.

For those new to streaming and digital media, there couldn't be a better time than now to get your feet wet. Technology vendors are now a bit more realistic, and prices for products and services have gone down. There are many examples of what has and has not worked, what the value is from these technologies, and how you can judge your success in the digital media arena.

4.2 You can avoid the top four mistakes made in the early days by understanding the business impact of licensing, security, distribution, and quality

The four basic components of a digital media business consist of licensing the technology, securing the content, distributing the content, and making sure the content is provided with the right quality metrics to either get the message across or deliver content for which users will be willing to pay.

Many companies chose to overlook these four factors, especially distribution and quality, and instead focused on their content. Companies thought that the content they were creating was so original that people would pay for it no matter the price or the quality. This was primarily the case in the media and entertainment vertical and when it came to the business-to-consumer (B2C) models. However, as these companies soon found out, without paying attention to all of the above mentioned components, they could not survive as a successful business model.

4.3 Don't let your strategy get sidetracked by the media player market share numbers

Don't let your strategy get sidetracked by hype of other companies. It seems that every few quarters one company puts out a third-party report saying they have a bigger piece of the market, and then a competing platform puts out a similar report saying that they have the lead. Of course if you ask any of the big three, Microsoft, RealNetworks, or Apple, they will tell you exactly how many systems they have installed and what percentage of the market they have. What they don't tell you is the version of all those players they have installed and exactly how many "unique" end users they are reaching. For example, I have three computers and if I download a RealNetworks media player on all three machines, the company counts that as three downloads, but I am only one user. The amount of players each platform has installed in the market on end users' computers is one of the biggest unsolved questions in the industry; however, you don't need to know those numbers or get caught up in all the marketing hype to be successful.

The Aberdeen and StreamingMedia.com surveys both asked respondents the following question: Which of the following media players do you have installed on your desktop? (check all that apply):

a. Windows Media Player from Microsoft
b. RealPlayer from RealNetworks
c. QuickTime Player from Apple
d. MPEG player
e. Customized player
f. Other

Figure 4.1 summarizes the responses to the surveys.

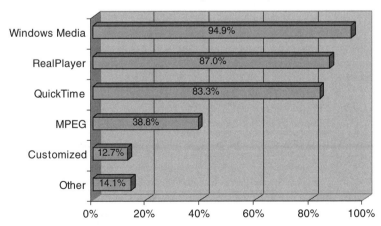

A9. Which of the following media players do you have installed on your desktop?

Figure 4.1: *Uses of Streaming and Digital Media, report published in 2004 by streamingmedia.com/Aberdeen.*

Microsoft has the highest installed penetration among respondents; nearly 95 percent reported that Windows Media Player is installed on their desktops. RealPlayer is close behind with an 87 percent installed base, and QuickTime has 83 percent. MPEG players are installed on nearly 39 percent of desktops, and customized players are installed on less than 13 percent.

Analysis—Most users have several media players installed.

Impact—Aberdeen research shows that, behind the firewall, most companies choose one format and require their users to view content in that format. The high installed base of all three players, Microsoft, RealPlayer, and QuickTime, guarantees that choosing any one of these formats will address a broad base of users who already have the player available. Companies that want to please the largest number of current users and deliver content in the widest preferred format should offer their content in the Microsoft format. Without multiple surveys conducted over several intervals, it is impossible to determine if any of the players' installed bases are growing or shrinking.

The Aberdeen survey asked respondents the following question: If given a choice, which format do you prefer to use? (check only one):

a. MPEG player
b. QuickTime (Apple)
c. RealMedia (RealNetworks)
d. Windows Media (Microsoft)
e. Other

Microsoft has a significant lead. QuickTime and RealPlayer have practically equal findings. Microsoft was selected as the preferred player by 40 percent of respondents. RealPlayer edged out QuickTime for second place, as these players finished with 22 and 21 percent, respectively. MPEG players garnered only 12 percent of player preference.

Figure 4.2 summarizes the aggregated responses to the survey.

Analysis—Microsoft is clearly the player of choice and has the highest penetration rate. The near even split between RealPlayer and QuickTime is interesting but only a starting point for further research. Tracking this question over time will provide better insight into whether Apple will overtake RealNetworks, or if format preferences have reached stabilization.

Impact—When combined with the installed base results, this question reinforces the recommendation that enterprises and content providers that seek to reach the widest possible audience should use Windows Media format. RealPlayer and QuickTime are also important options, particularly for content providers trying to please the majority of the potential user base.

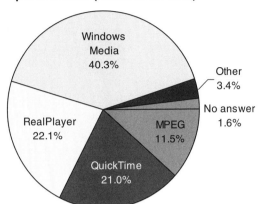

A10. If given a choice, which format do you prefer to use? (Check ONLY ONE)

Figure 4.2: *Uses of Streaming and Digital Media, report published in 2004 by streamingmedia.com/Aberdeen.*

4.3.1 There are no agreed upon or default standards for platforms—yet

When it comes to deciding on a digital media strategy, many people find it difficult to decide which codec, platform, or technology to distribute their content in. Because of the lack of standards in the marketplace and the public relations and marketing hype from many technology companies, there are many choices. But choosing a specific codec or platform is something that must be done, and it should be the easiest part of the entire digital media process.

As noted above, Microsoft Windows Media Player, RealNetworks' RealPlayer, and Apple's QuickTime platforms account for nearly 99 percent of the market share of the streaming media formats. Many companies spend a great deal of time and resources in choosing their platform and spend less time focusing on their business model strategy or quality of content. Although technology does play a part in your strategy, knowing a few key things about platforms will prevent a lot of headaches.

First, realize that a lot of what the platform providers do is tell you about the best possible quality their platforms can produce, yet this is usually never what you need or what your end users are capable of receiving. Although all of the platforms do broadcast quality streams, surround sound, and in some cases high definition, not many end users have the ability to receive content of that quality. It seems that everyone has a different opinion of what platform has the best compression for audio or video and who has the most players installed capable of reaching the most end users.

With that said, nearly everyone in the industry agrees on these facts. Microsoft Windows Media, which comes bundled with Microsoft's operating system in the United States, means that most Fortune 1000 corporations who are primarily Windows based have a version of the Windows Media Player already on their desktop. Because nearly every enterprise corporation runs on a Windows environment, Microsoft is the clear leader in the enterprise space in terms of market share. Their server technology also incorporates many aspects of DRM and other underlying streaming media technologies seamlessly, which makes deploying streaming and digital media easier.

RealNetworks, which used to have the largest market share for its player and was the first streaming media platform in the industry, has since focused on becoming more of a content company and less of a technology company. In the wireless arena they still focus heavily on deploying their technology instead of content with cell phone carriers. Their business model used to rely solely on licensing its server technology to allow corporations and service providers to distribute streaming media in the RealNetworks format. Since 2001, RealNetworks has moved away from server license fees as its primary means of revenue and has embraced a content revenue model that offers subscription-based services for exclusive content and downloadable music. This has angered some content providers who are also trying to establish a business model for Web-based subscription services. They feel it is unfair that they are competing against the developers of the technology platform.

Apple's QuickTime technology, which has been around since the beginning, originally in a non-streaming format, is still primarily used by Web producers, DVD and CD-ROM authors, and those who are looking to provide content via a download as opposed to streaming media. QuickTime has the majority share of the market when it comes to DVD- and CD-ROM-based media, but very little market share when it comes to live webcast content. They have players on the market, but the content providers don't produce as much content in the QuickTime format as Windows Media or RealNetworks. A quick search of the Web shows that any content in the QuickTime format is rarely broadcast live.

4.3.2 Understanding the impact of Windows Media, RealNetworks, and MPEG licensing plans on your business

Now that you know what is available in the platform arena, understanding the impact of their licensing fees on your business is crucial. Microsoft Windows Media server is free but must be installed on a Microsoft server.

Microsoft makes it money off the .NET or XP server license you buy as Windows Media obviously only works on a Windows-based server. Microsoft is a software company and, hence, its entire revenue comes from selling software. RealNetworks still has a license model whereby you must purchase a server license based on the number of simultaneous streams you want to deliver at any given time. Its newest platform, Helix, is an open-source platform and its server software can be installed on just about every operation system including Linux. The QuickTime server and its components are all free, and it is also an open-source product.

The impact of these licensing plans is crucial to understand, especially when streaming from within your organization on your own network. However, if you are outsourcing streaming media delivery to a service provider or content delivery network (CDN), there is typically no additional cost to you no matter what format you choose. This service is free because the provider has already purchased licenses from the respected platforms and then resells the hosting service and bundles that license fee into their cost to the consumer.

The cost to purchase a .NET server license to install Windows Media usually costs a few thousand dollars. A typical net server, consisting of a single processor and a gig of memory, can typically push out thousands of concurrent streams. The RealNetworks server license can cost as much as six figures a year to be able to push out the same amount of simultaneous streams as a Windows server. However, as RealNetworks continues to evolve toward content as opposed to server fees, its pricing continues to drop. Apple's QuickTime streaming server is included as part of the Mac OS X Server, which costs between $500 to $1,000, depending on the selected options (www.apple.com/server/macosx/).

A different licensing model is used with MPEG-4. This is an ISO/IEC standard developed by Moving Picture Experts Group (MPEG), the committee that also developed the Emmy Award-winning standards known as MPEG-1 and MPEG-2. These standards made interactive video on CD-ROM and digital television possible. MPEG-4 is the result of another international effort involving hundreds of researchers and engineers from all over the world. MPEG-4 was finalized in October 1998 and became an international standard in the beginning of 1999.

MPEG-4 builds on the proven success of three fields: (1) digital television, (2) interactive graphics applications (synthetic content), and (3) interactive multimedia (World Wide Web, distribution of and access to content). It provides the standardized technological elements that allow integration of the production, distribution, and content access paradigms of the above three fields. MPEG-4 probably has one of the most confusing licensing models in the marketplace. To help navigate the licensing mode, it is best to visit www.m4if.org, which gives a number of links and information about the different types of licensing programs available.

4.3.3 Why you might need multiple formats, encoding rates, etc.

How do you pick and choose which formats and platforms are right for you? Are there times when one format is needed more than another, or multiple formats and encoding rates can be used? Typically, the format and encoding bit rate in which you choose to encode and deliver content is based on the demographics of your target end users as well as their connection speed to the Internet. For instance, if an organization is deploying streaming media content and knows that everyone is running a Windows-based desktop, it might elect to choose just the Windows Media format to encode and distribute their content. Because the streaming is internal, the connection speed of the average end user is known. This enables the organization to encode the content at a specific bit rate just for that targeted end user. The majority of corporate communications content that is broadcast internally is usually encoded between 80 to 100 Kbps.

For content that is streamed outside a network, an organization may elect to encode it at 56 Kbps for users that might be outside of the office or traveling and only have access to a dial-up connection. As you will read later in Chapter 5, some content only needs to be encoded at a certain bit rate and is sufficient at that bit rate even when more bandwidth may be available. Utilizing any form of streaming or digital media technology is not about showcasing the most cutting-edge advancement or quality in the platforms; instead it is about using the technology that is best suited for the content and the end user.

For instances where you are not sure of your end-user's connection to the Internet or format of choice they prefer, many companies elect to encode and deliver their content in the Microsoft Windows Media format and RealNetworks format at both narrowband (56 Kbps) and broadband (300 Kbps). The biggest impact this has on your business is the fact that it will take you longer to encode your content in dual formats rather than a single format. It also means that you are storing twice the amount of data, which may not be a problem if you are hosting it yourself and have excess storage. However, it would cost you more money if you were hosting your content with a service provider.

As a general rule, if end users want the content badly enough and do not have a player on their computer in the selected format, they will go and download that platform. However, that is not a given in the industry. There is no standard and if it is crucial for you to reach every user in every format and at both narrow- and broadband, be prepared to spend more money and more time to do so. No matter what platform you implement, you should closely monitor what the preferred platform is on your Web site, who your target end user is, and what the average connection speed is. You can always tailor your business later by electing to go with just one format after you have evaluated the situation. If there is one thing to remember from reading this book, it is that you don't need to spend a lot of time, a lot of money, or a lot of resources to simply evaluate what is possible with streaming and digital media technology. If you're not sure, don't try to put your entire library online. Start with a small focused sample group of content and, after a few months, you will be able to judge your success in terms of reaching the right end user with the right technology and platform.

4.4 The changing value of CDNs for streaming and digital media distribution

For all of the advances in the streaming media industry over the years, the most commonly asked and confusing question corporations still face is how to pick the right service provider or Content Delivery Network (CDN). A CDN is a company that allows you to rent space on their servers and bandwidth on their network. Using a CDN means you don't have to purchase, set up, or maintain your own servers and software necessary to deliver your content.

Since the introduction of CDNs, the models by which their services are marketed, priced, and delivered have changed faster than any aspect of this business. The perception for the need to use a CDN has grown as well. In the early days of the Internet, most CDN providers focused on placing many small servers at many locations throughout the world. The assumption at the time was that there would be such a demand for the content that CDNs could place the content as close as possible to the end user and deliver a better quality experience. For a few years this notion was considered to be industry standard, until the bubble burst. People were not consuming rich media in the numbers that were advertised and companies had built such excess that excess amounts of server capacity existed. Companies such as Akamai rushed to still confirm to the industry that "quantity" equaled "quality" when it came to the number of servers a CDN had deployed. Since then, many

CDN providers like Mirror Image and Speedera have chosen to simply deploy larger boxes at fewer locations and still have managed to deliver the same quality. No matter who you ask, it seems each person has a different opinion on which CDN has the best network or technical set up, but the fact remains that the services CDNs offer—storage and bandwidth—are now commodities in the marketplace.

Choosing the right CDN provider still continues to be a difficult task. Outsourcing all or part of the process can leave you with more questions than answers', which we cover in chapter 6.

4.5 The most common outsourced application—live webcasting

One of the most common streaming media applications outsourced by corporations to CDNs is live webcasting. Like the rest of the streaming media services offered today, a live webcasting component is one that varies from one provider to another and tends to have people asking a lot of questions.

Utilizing streaming media technology in a live environment is a great way to take advantage of global communication at a fraction of the cost of traditional broadcast mediums. When making the decision to use the Internet to broadcast your message, there are many decisions to make. Some corporations have the in-house resources to make the broadcast happen, but most companies need to outsource the live event to a service provider.

4.5.1 Understanding the basics

Understanding what is involved in a live event from a technical perspective is important, as the technical resources chosen will be the biggest factor in the event cost and complexity. Typically, a live event is broken down into five main components:

1. Audio and/or video capture
2. Signal acquisition/transmit
3. Content encoding
4. Delivery or distribution
5. Web site interface integration

The first piece of any live event is audio and video content. Some events consist of just an audio component, such as a quarterly investors' relations call, while others consist of video as well as audio. The first step in any live event is the ability to record and film the content, otherwise known as "capture." This factor can be one of the highest costs depending on the complexity of the capture needs.

Once the audio/video content is captured, the signal needs to be transmitted to the location where it will be encoded. Depending on the event, this process is can be done a few different ways. The signal can be sent to a satellite in the sky (typically referred to as "uplinking") where it is then pulled down (otherwise known as "downlinking") at the service provider's offices for encoding. Another way to capture the signal is via a phone bridge, which can be done if the live event content consists of just a conference call. The signal can also be sent via connectivity at the event location if the content is encoded on site from the venue.

After the signal has been acquired via satellite, phone bridge, or another method, it needs to be encoded for distribution over the Internet. Encoding the content consists of taking the audio/video signal and transforming it into a streaming media file format ready for Internet distribution. Windows Media, RealMedia, and QuickTime are names for these formats. Encoding is done by using an "encoder," a hardware-based device with capture cards and software that allows the signal to be digitized into one of the above mentioned file formats.

Now that the content has been captured, acquired, and encoded, it is ready for delivery, which is also referred to as "distribution." Once the signal is encoded, it is sent to servers sitting on a delivery network that transmit the content to viewers via the Internet. For most service providers, the distribution of your content on the Internet is the largest cost associated with a live event. Understanding the components that affect the costs for these services will allow you to make sure you don't pay for delivery bandwidth you don't use.

Another technical piece that can typically be involved in broadcasts is Web site integration or interactivity. Live broadcasts on the Internet have the ability to include interactive functions such as chat, polling, and PowerPoint slides. Additionally, the service provider can build a micro Web site on which to host the event as well as additional options such as setting up a registration interface that allows you to collect user data. Many options are available when it comes to interactivity, and the complexity and amount of options chosen will affect the final cost for technical services.

4.5.2 Determining your business needs

Now that you know what is involved in the broadcast, the next step is to decide on the technical needs of your webcast. Depending on your needs and the type of broadcast taking place, webcasting your live event can be very simple or very complex. The scope and scale of the above five components will determine the cost and resources needed to pull off a successful webcast. But before you answer the technical questions, you should ask yourself some business questions: (1) Does the event need to be live?, (2) Who is your target audience?, and (3) How do you plan on measuring your return on investment?

While broadcasting your content live has its advantages, it is also more expensive than simply recording it and archiving it for later use. Many times the nature of the content justifies a live broadcast, such as breaking news, a corporate announcement, or an investors' relations call. However, if the content is not of a time-sensitive nature, you may want to reconsider allocating the resources and budget of live broadcasting and seek other options from the service provider.

Who is your target audience? Understanding these demographics is crucial to a successful webcast. You can have a flawlessly produced broadcast from a technical standpoint, but it can fail if it doesn't deliver the message you want to convey to the people you want to watch it. When preparing to webcast your content, figure out who your ideal end user is. Knowing the time, physical location, and way end users will be able to access the broadcast is essential. This will also be a huge question when we talk about factors that affect the cost of the webcast.

Whether you spend $1,000 or 10,000 on a webcast, no investment is worth the money if you are not prepared to judge how successful it was. Having a defined set of parameters that allows you to see your return on investment (ROI) is essential. A large portion of the ROI is usually based on the metrics delivered after the webcast by the service provider. These reports (also known as "reporting") vary based on the distribution service provider. Typically, these reports tell you how many people watched your broadcast and the average length they viewed. You should also judge the metrics based on the quality of the message you delivered. Was it clear, concise, and delivered in the format and way you wanted? Also, if you made your viewers preregister before the event by filling in their contact information, you have the ability to send them a follow-up questionnaire asking for feedback. This is another great way to measure the effectiveness of your webcast. While live webcasts can vary from one another based on the scope, size, and components included, understanding these variables is the first step in broadcasting a successful live webcast on the Internet.

4.5.3 The bigger picture

You should now be aware that a good service provider, one who takes the time to understand your needs, can help make your company's communications needs a reality. Service providers can help your company achieve real-world communication solutions with interactivity that allows you to communicate on a global basis at a fraction of the cost of traditional communications. Improved efficiency and enhanced effective communication of the message you are delivering is what choosing a good provider is all about.

The CDN model has evolved over the years and will continue evolving as we see this technology leveraged into mainstream applications. Picking a service provider will always continue to be tricky, because the needs of each corporation vary and the solutions offered continue to change every year as the technology advances. But if you continue to educate yourself, ask questions, and set realistic expectations, the process of choosing a service provider will be much easier.

4.6 Quality is so important it deserves its own chapter—Chapter 5

You must focus on the quality of the content you are delivering. Without this focus, you are setting your streaming or digital media business up for failure. Whether you're delivering content from your organization or using an external CDN or service provider, you must determine what type of quality is required for the type of content you are delivering and the end user who is consuming it. Probably the biggest myth when it comes to service providers is who offers the best "quality." When talking about quality, remember that the quality of the service is not always based on one factor, but is usually based on a variety of factors such as speed, ease of use, price, scalability, and customer service. Chapter 5 discusses how to determine what level of quality you should expect.

4.7 Case studies

4.7.1 Bumble and bumble

Between its founding in 1977 and early 2003, Bumble and bumble, a boutique manufacturer and marketer of hair-care products, had established a close relationship with its nearly 1,500 salon partners across the United States. The company emphasized "great hairdressing and great PR" as the keys to a successful business in the hair-care industry. The company knew that the most effective way to ensure its products were promoted by salons was to train salon stylists and customers about hairdressing and the benefits of using Bumble and bumble products in achieving great looks.

However, stylist training is not a scalable task: Stylists need hands-on experience to learn these techniques, and they benefit greatly from close-up views of live demonstrations. The company regularly mailed DVDs to partner salons, but based on surveys, Bumble and bumble thought that only about 20 percent of the stylists actually watched the videos.

The solution

The company took three specific steps to raise its contact with partner salons and increase the training around Bumble and bumble products. First, the company designed and built a new corporate headquarters in lower Manhattan, two floors of which were dedicated to "Bumble and bumble University," a world-class stylist training facility. Bumble and bumble developed a campaign that linked quality training with the company's products. Salons earned points by selling products, which were then redeemed for courses at "Bb.U."

Second, the building design included a pervasive, dedicated digital media network. Video cameras were installed in each classroom, with two 6 × 6-foot projection screens next to the instructor platforms. Close-up cameras streamed images of instructor's techniques to in-class projectors. The system was designed so that instructors could coordinate the in-class video usage themselves. With the help of a video-savvy integrator, Bumble and bumble built a customized command and control application that sits on PowerMac laptops.

Third, all classroom video content could be streamed to a video production studio where it could be recorded and stored in a digital media archive. If they wanted to, instructors could call up previous sessions or examples on the in-class monitors as well show how other stylists used different techniques.

In addition to these training-focused initiatives, Bumble and bumble also wanted to leverage its creative department's media-driven marketing. Stylists coming for training saw the marketing videos on monitors that were installed throughout the building—in the lobby, office suites, and public areas—to stream messages and promotion about the company and its products.

Finally, the company installed monitors in the two salons it owns and operates in New York City. Point-of-purchase displays and overhead monitors were networked to the main data center. Marketing videos were streamed to the salon entrance and above the stylist stations, which included over the customer's head during shampooing.

The benefit to Bumble and bumble

When it opened in April 2004, Bumble and bumble's new headquarters and Bb.U instantly raised the level of stylist training and strengthened the connection between company and salon partners. The impact on stylist involvement with Bumble and bumble products is unquestioned: Over one thousand students have come through the programs, and the courses are booked solid for the next six months. The company's director of new media said, "The use of video has put us into another league in terms of customer perception. Everyone that walks in says we're much bigger than they expected, due to the sophistication of our media presentations."

Video has had an impact within the company as well. The director continued, "More people within the business are starting to see film and video as required, instead of optional. Before, they may have just used PowerPoint, but now they want to include video in almost all of their presentations. That's largely due to the level of quality of the presentations they do see, which raises the quality level of each and every meeting." In some ways, the company is suffering from being too successful with its video usage. "We're fighting people's expectations a lot: They think it's going to be like TV, with movie stars and high production values. Just the presence of a screen raises the expectations."

In the near future

Bumble and bumble expects the demand for internal and external video use to increase in the next year by at least 50 percent over the current level. The rapid growth of video usage is also causing some production and monitoring challenges, particularly around content management and measuring viewership. Overcoming these challenges is just a part of daily life for companies integrating digital media so closely into their core capabilities. Bumble and bumble is looking for strategies to reach more of its salon partners on a dynamic and regular basis. The director of new media said, "Eventually, I want to have point-of-sale monitors in every salon, and have them all networked with streaming content. That way, we can change the content more frequently and we can better coordinate the marketing content for new product launches."

4.7.2 New York City public schools

New York City wanted to link its K–12 schools together with each other and with important cultural institutions in the city. They sought a system that would go beyond using a high-quality one- and two-way video system but still enable classes in the five boroughs to share in presentations and special events. In addition the system must allow the students to undertake "virtual field trips" to cultural treasures like the Lincoln Center Institute and the American Museum of Natural History, all without leaving the safety of the classroom. They needed a system that moved beyond the poor quality video common in ISDN-based video-conferencing systems. A successful system had to offer television quality video and sound—anything else would be too distracting for students raised to expect TV quality video at all times. Because the system would be administered by educators, it needed to be easy to deploy and easy to use on a regular basis. With a limited budget, it also needed to leverage the city's extensive IP network.

The solution

After assessing various possible suppliers, the City of New York turned to VBrick Systems. Their video systems are used by everyone from the White House to the Utah education network. For this project, the VBrick 6200 MPEG-2 encoder/decoder and VBrick 5300 dual decoder were used to link the first of 33 distance learning classrooms made up of 17 Board of Education schools, 5 CUNY colleges, 8 city employee training centers, and 3 content providers. The MPEG-2 video compression provided DVD-quality video and sound that ensured the vital sense of "continuous presence," which provided a more natural communication experience for everyone.

At a typical school, VBricks are attached to TV monitors, which give the students a seamless, simultaneous discussion with three other schools. Presentations, lectures, and even satellite feeds are scheduled using TODD Video Network Management software and can be arranged on demand or pre-scheduled to automatically connect specific schools on a time-of-day or day-of-week basis. A central administrator can easily make the connections over the city's IP network. The compact and portable VBricks, no larger than an average DVD player, are used on mobile carts in the American Museum of Natural History and the Lincoln Center Institute to broadcast both one- and two-way virtual field trips to these and other cultural institutions. Even WNYE, the Board of Education Television station, uses VBrick 4300 dual encoders in its three sound production stages and to stream satellite feeds containing educational programs to I-NET sites, which in turn distribute the live video to classrooms.

The benefit

This innovative system connecting schools and cultural institutions offers a number of important benefits. Students can take advantage of lectures and

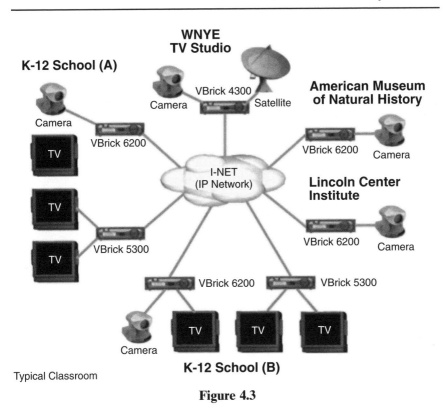

Figure 4.3

presentations without traveling to other schools. The system also breaks down barriers by connecting students with different backgrounds to each other. For educators, this easy-to-use, high-quality video system enhances the learning experience for their students by reaching beyond the walls of the classroom and opening up the rich cultural heritage of New York.

Another important benefit is that modern video-conferencing systems like that from VBrick Systems, which leverage the existing broadband network infrastructure. The city of New York has saved millions of dollars by using its existing I-NET network to link schools by video rather than spending its scarce resources on new, unnecessary network infrastructure.

With VBrick Systems' smart, powerful, and affordable operation, educators in New York City are realizing the long overdue promise of video as an effective education tool.

CHAPTER 5

Quality and Content Are King and Queen of the Digital Media Realm

5.1 If you don't have good content or sufficient quality, don't bother

Since content was first delivered on the Internet, the debate has always raged whether content or quality was king. Ten years later, after the inception of streaming media technology, quality and content are king and queen and can't coexist without each other. You can have great content and horrible quality and your message won't get through. On the other hand, you can have a high quality, well-produced video comprised of terrible content and your message will be missed. This chapter discusses how to control quality, the factors that affect quality, and what to think about when developing or re-purposing content for the Internet.

5.2 The definitions of "good content" and "sufficient quality" change depending upon your target audience, usage, price charged, etc.

Before starting any digital media strategy, the first step is to evaluate the type and quality of the content you have or will be producing. The nature of the content will be a big deciding factor on the quality that is achieved. Video content that has less motion and no quick pans, like a press conference of someone standing behind a podium, is naturally going to look better based on the way streaming media technology works than, for instance, video of a sporting event with quick movement. While you can still achieve great quality of high motion content, chances are you'll need to increase the frame rate and size of the file. This makes it possible for users with broadband access to achieve the quality that you desire and that end users expect. The main goal of any digital media undertaking is always to deliver the best possible content at the highest possible quality. When thinking about how to present your content on the Web, realize that in most cases the typical viewer watches five minutes or less per video clip of typical Web video. Decide what sections are most important and highlight them. Try to edit your content so that it can be viewed in small, manageable sections, which allows viewers to be able to walk away with the clear and concise message you want to deliver. To do this, always start with a high-quality source for your content. Digital media content is like a fax, the more times you copy it, the more distorted it becomes. Using the original source at the highest possible quality ensures the best possible quality when it comes to encoding. If you don't have a plan for what content to use, and how to guarantee its quality, you are setting yourself up for failure with any digital media undertaking.

Streaming media quality is so widely acknowledged to be important that in 2003 there were at least three independent companies who specialized in measuring the quality of streaming media delivery. One company, Keynote, is considered the global leader in Web performance measurement, and its testing and management services recently added a streaming-media-based quality of service (QOS) offering. In 2003, streaming media quality measurement was so in demand that Keynote acquired a Toronto-based company called Streamcheck and integrated its offering into their suite of solutions. Until now, no independent third-party company ever offered a QOS product that allowed corporations to measure their delivery quality or that of a CDNs.

Keynote's Streaming Perspective is a Web-based, automated service that measures the quality and reliability of streaming media delivery from the end-user perspective. It gives reports on buffering delays or broken links. For companies streaming live content, Streaming Perspective can be an early warning system when an encoder is down. If you have on-demand content, Streaming Perspective will tell you whether you need to add server capacity, a caching system, or perhaps switch to an outsourced delivery provider. If you have already outsourced your stream hosting, you can also use Streaming Perspective to ensure that your hosting provider is living up to its service level agreement (SLA).

5.2.1 How Streaming Perspective works

Streaming Perspective works by measuring audio and video streams from multiple locations throughout the United States, Japan, and Europe. This is done by using measurement computers called "agents." These agents attempt to connect to your streams 10 times per hour. Once connected, the agent will play your content for 60 seconds while recording the following data:

- Network statistics (e.g., DNS time, trace routes, packet statistics)
- Streaming statistics (e.g., connection success rate, bit rate, connect/buffer/ re-buffer time)
- Server statistics (e.g., server type, serving platform, streaming protocol)
- Presentation statistics (e.g., frame rate, player errors, metafiles, and URLs)
- Increased checking frequencies and longer check durations are also available upon request

At the heart of Keynote's Streaming Perspective service is a network of measurement agents distributed throughout Europe, Canada, and the United States. These agents are connected to the public Internet and run proprietary software that mimics the behavior of a streaming client such as RealPlayer or Windows Media Player.

5.3 Some content is excellent for streaming or digital media, while others are unsuitable

The biggest thing to keep in mind when reading this chapter is that many people define quality differently. Some people think of quality as a large-sized video window, others by the smoothness of the videos, others how quickly they can receive the content, and some folks judge quality on all of the above—or none of the above. Many times, consumers tend to judge quality based on cost and availability and will overlook technology or bit rate. However, remember that the quality of the content should be based primarily on two factors: (1) what does your end user expect in terms of quality and what expectations have you set and how best should you go about achieving them, and (2) selecting the determining factors to judge what quality means, based on the content used.

Use the right technology for the right application. For example, you can encode an audio-only stream at 100 Kbps, but the same audio stream, encoded at half that size, is going to sound almost identical to the higher bit rate stream. In fact, most users won't be able to notice a quality difference in terms of audio clarity from a 50- to 100-Kbps audio stream. The reason for this is that audio content doesn't need to be encoded at a high bit rate in order to have clear, well-defined audio.

Years ago, users on the Internet complained that many movie preview trailers are generally encoded at such high bit rates that it can take 20 minutes just to download a 30-second movie file. Many of the studios believe that they need to encode the trailers at such a high bit rate so they can make the experience as close to going to a movie as possible. Consumers don't expect to see a video file in the same high-quality format as a movie, nor are they going to skip going to see a movie just because their computers can't play back full-screen video. Understand what your end users expect and realize what the limitations are for quality versus accessibility. Understanding this is key.

5.3.1 Your content dictates the kind of technology you use, not the other way around

When it comes to choosing which content you want to distribute in your digital media strategy, it is important to remember that some content is great for the medium while others are unsuitable. The kind of content you have dictates the technology you use, not the other way around.

Content with quick motion such as sporting events may not be best suited for end users who do not have the ability to receive the stream at broadband connections. In the past, many companies would stream the content and hope that over time users would upgrade to broadband. However, companies like ESPN realized they could change their distribution strategy and still get high-quality, fast moving content to non-broadband users. ESPN changed the way it delivered the content by moving away from a stream and moving to a model that would download full-screen action clips to your desktop overnight after you left for the day. Users whose computers would sit idle at night would then have the clips saved to their machine, and when they came in the next day they would have full-screen, high-resolution video content to watch. ESPN's motion offering is a perfect example of how companies can determine the factors that will allow them to pick the best available digital media method to satisfy their consumers.

Even in the business to business (B2B) space the same principle applies. If you are distributing video of a talking head presentation, you could encode it at 300 Kbps and make it available on your network. However, you will quickly find that if you encode it at 80 Kbps instead, the quality will suffice for the medium and you will use nearly one-third the bandwidth and save on storage space based on the size of the file.

5.4 When determining the best quality for your company, make sure you understand the four sides of the digital media "business square"

As mentioned in previous chapters, the audience size accessing your content plays a big role in the cost and complexity of your digital media offering. When determining the best quality for your company, make sure you understand all four sides of the digital media business square: audience size, file size, encoding bit rate, and security. While the file size of your content, the bit rate at which it is encoded, and the security of your media are also just as important, the audience size you are trying to reach is usually the biggest unknown factor, especially when targeting consumers. Statistics vary, but some of the latest findings from Arbitron, an international media and marketing research firm that publishes media audience numbers, show that the number of users consuming audio and video content on the Internet continues to grow at an astronomical rate each month. Their report, published in 2004 showed that more than 1 out of 5 Americans, representing 50 million consumers age 12 and older, have used Internet audio or video in the past month.

This particular study, titled Internet and Multimedia 11: New Media Enters the Mainstream, also revealed that the long-standing model of free programming supported by advertising is preferred by Internet broadcast users. Given the choice between free programming with commercials, a small monthly fee with fewer commercials, or a higher monthly fee with no commercials:

- Sixty-one percent of people who listen to Internet audio and 59 percent of those who watch Internet video prefer free programming supported by advertising.
- Only 14 percent of Internet audio users preferred either of the two subscription choices.

- Twenty percent of Internet video users prefer paying a small monthly fee for programming with few commercials, and 12 percent prefer a higher monthly fee with no commercials.

Barberton's study found that Internet broadcasting is a strong medium for reaching early adopters, with 20 percent of them having tuned to Internet broadcasts in the past week. Overall, the weekly Internet broadcast audience is 50 percent more likely to be early adopters than the total population. Additional findings from the study include: (1) 80 percent of the total population now has access to the Internet from any location, up from 75 percent in the Arbitron/Edison Media Research survey of January 2003; and (2) the number of Americans with residential broadband Internet access has tripled since January 2001, rising to 21 percent as of July 2003. One-third of early adopters live in homes with residential broadband.

Although these findings don't give the exact number of potential Internet users you may be looking to reach, they do give you a good indication that the potential market for digital media businesses who are looking to deliver content to the widest possible audience continues to grow every month. Based on the size of your audience, or potential audience, the cost for delivering your content can fluctuate from one month to another based on the amount of usage. For corporations utilizing streaming media to deliver content to employees, partners, or re-sellers, digital media consumption numbers are pretty easy to figure out because you know exactly how many end users you have in your organization. It's when you are delivering content to an external audience of unknown size that your monthly bill can double or triple each month based on the volume of users.

One way to figure out this cost is by knowing your file size. This is the amount of bandwidth that is used to transmit your content from your server or network to end users on the Internet. The size of your file is determined by the content's digitized bit rate before it can be delivered via the Internet. By calculating the content's bit rate, the length of the file, and the estimated number of users who will watch the content, you can figure out the amount of bandwidth that will be utilized each month and how much you will be charged if this content is delivered through a service provider. The chart below helps to explain the process.

5.4.1 Calculating bandwidth chart based on user consumption

Delivering content on the Web requires an understanding of how bandwidth is calculated. Knowing how much bandwidth you sustain and how many bits you deliver allows you to determine what your CDN will charge every month and what you can sustain when you are streaming internally on your internal infrastructure.

Understanding the basics

Digitized bits of information are commonly transmitted across fiber-optic strands of glass, or copper wires, measured in "bits per second" (a bit is always abbreviated by the lowercase b):

Common term	Symbol	Definition
Bit	B	1 bit
Kilobit	Kb	1,000 bits (thousands)
Megabit	Mb	1,000,000 (millions)
Terabit	Gb	1,000,000,000 (billions)

When bits are stored for later use they are grouped together eight at a time creating a unit of measure called a byte (a byte is always abbreviated by an uppercase B):

Common term	Symbol	Definition
Kilobits per second	Kbps	1 bit
Megabits per second	Mbps	1,000 (thousands)
Gigabits per second	Gbps	1,000,000 (millions)
Terabits per second	Tbps	1,000,000,000 (billions)

When these bytes are transferred across the same fiber-optic strands as mentioned above, they are measured as "bytes transferred" or "bytes delivered."

Common term	Symbol	Definition
Byte	Byte	8 bit
Kilobyte	KB	8,000 bits
Megabyte	MB	8,000,000 bits
Gigabyte	GB	8,000,000,000 bits
Terabyte	TB	8,000,000,000,000 bits

Calculating bandwidth based on bit rate

In order to know how much bandwidth you are using, you need to understand streaming bit rates. Most service providers calculate bandwidth usage based on a kilobits per second model. In the streaming world, most people refer to the bit rate they are encoding at as 14.4, 28.8, 56k, and broadband. But it is important to know that these do not represent the "actual" kilobits per second at which the content is being encoded. For instance, when encoding for a user accessing content via a 56-k modem, the actual content is usually encoded between 37 and 40Kbps. This happens so that there is a "buffer" that allows users who may not get a true 56-Kbps dial-up from their ISP to still be able to access the content.

Once you know the actual kilobits per second of the content that you are delivering, to figure out your bandwidth multiply Kbps × length of content × number of users.

Connect speed (kb/s)		Actual (Mb/s)		MB/min	MB transferred/HR
28.8 k	20	0.020	0.0025	0.150	9.0
56 k	37	0.037	0.0046	0.278	16.7
100 k	80	0.080	0.0100	0.600	36.0
T1/cable	300	0.300	0.0375	2.250	135.0

The numbers in the above chart are theoretical maximums. SureStream files add all bit rates together (i.e., a SureStream file with 28-, 56-, and 100-k streams is the same as three separate files). Windows Media and QuickTime files can be smaller due to variable compression codecs.

Bandwidth example

A broadcaster does a scheduled broadcast five days a week, two hours a day, for a month. The station is sending its CDN provider an encoded stream at 56 and 100k. One hundred users are expected to be connected at all times. The first thing you need to do is have an idea of the connection speed of the end users. Let's figure there will be 50 percent accessing the 100-k stream and the other 50 percent connecting at 56k.

Looking at the chart above you will see that in one hour a 100-k stream will transfer 36MB. If they are doing a two-hour show once a day, then in two hours one user will transfer 72MB. Then multiply that 72MB per day for one user × the 20 weekdays in the month. That gives a total of 1,440MB a month transfer for one user. Now remember that 100 users are expected, 50 percent of which we determined were going to access the 100-k file. Then take the 1440MB and multiply by 50 users (50 users is 50 percent of the total 100 users the broadcaster says it will have). 1,440MB × 50 = 72,000MB. This is the total amount of data that will be transferred for 50 people accessing the 100-k stream for 2 hours a day, 5 days a week, for 1 month.

Now let's look at the other 50 percent connecting at 56 k. From the chart you will see that in one hour a 56-k stream will transfer 16.7 MB. If they are doing a two-hour show once a day, then in two hours one user will transfer 33.4 MB. Then multiply that 33.4 MB per day for one user × the 20 days of the week in the month. That gives you a total of 668 MB a month transfer for one user. Now remember that the station is expecting 100 users, 50 percent of which we determined were going to access the 56-k file. So take the 668 MB and multiply by 50 users (50 users is 50 percent of the total 100 users the broadcaster says it will have). 668 MB × 50 = 33,400 MB. This is the total amount of data that will be transferred for 50 people accessing the 56-k stream for 2 hours a day, 5 days a week, for 1 month.

Total transfer is 72,000 MB for the 100 k + 33,400 MB for the 56 k. Total MB transferred = 105,400 MB. If you are paying, for example, $0.01 per megabit delivered then you would multiply 105,400 × $0.01. This adds up to spending $1,054 a month for delivery charges.

Now that you understand the basics of calculating bandwidth, determining your bandwidth usage will allow you to better measure your ROI and estimate what distributing your digital media will cost. Keep in mind this is just an example and depending on the deal you have structured with your provider, you may pay more or less for delivery depending on the volume of data delivered and your level of commitment.

When it comes to nonconsumer-based streaming media, distance learning, and corporate communications, streaming with presentations is essential. The Gartner Group (www.gartner.com) estimated that over 21,000 businesses used some form of streaming media in 2001 and projected that the number of businesses using streaming media will exceed 225,000 in 2005. Getting corporations to adopt the streaming media technology as their core means of corporate communications will continue to grow as products that make the technology simpler penetrate the market.

5.5 If you change audience size, then you'll have to change your delivery strategy

As you can see from the just mentioned bandwidth charts, the audience size plays a crucial factor in how best to deliver your content. Depending on the size of your audience, different strategies can be applied to deliver content, be it live or on-demand, that will help you be more efficient and successful. For example, you have a global audience of 10,000 users who need to receive rich-media-based content within a short time period. If the content doesn't need to be live, you can deliver the content via a stream from your streaming media server, a download off of your Web site server, or cache that file close to the end user using an outsourced CDN provider. The best delivery method is not necessarily one of speed, ease of use, cost, or reliability; rather it is a factor of all of those combined. Your digital media strategy is a success because no one decision implemented by your plan was based on just one aspect.

5.6 Content size does matter when it comes to streaming and digital media

As discussed earlier, size of content (length) does matter when delivering via the Internet. Not only does it affect your cost to deliver as longer content takes up more bandwidth and storage, but also the length of the video or audio clip generally determines how long the end user will interact. Unlike years ago, today's technology allows even long video and audio clips to be searchable, indexed, and archived in such a way that users can jump to any point in the video. Unless you are going to apply search and indexing techniques to your content, most rich-media delivery is done with clips between 5 and 7 minutes long. For clips that are tied into e-commerce functionality where the company selling products wants to entice the consumer to buy, clips are usually less than 60 seconds long.

5.6.1 Session length of streaming and digital media

The Aberdeen and StreamingMedia.com survey asked respondents: How long is your typical session when using streaming or digital media? The answer choices were the following:

a. Less than 5 minutes
b. 5 to 15 minutes
c. 15 to 30 minutes
d. 30 minutes to 1 hour
e. 1 to 2 hours
f. More than 2 hours

Research found that 48 percent of respondents indicated that they use streaming or digital media for 15 minutes or less per session. Nearly 65

A2. How long is your typical session when using streaming or digital media? (All)

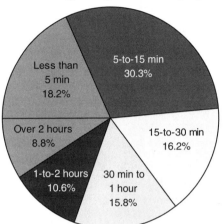

Figure 5.1: *(From Uses of Streaming and Digital Media, report published in 2004 by streamingmedia.com/Aberdeen.)*

percent of respondents said that they spend 30 minutes or less per session. Only 19.4 percent will spend more than 1 hour per session (Figure 5.1). Research analysis revealed that users are currently conditioned to consume short-format audio and video over IP networks. It is not clear from the research whether this results from a chicken-and-the-egg problem: Do respondents use short-format because they prefer it or because that is all that is available? The impact of these findings is somewhat uncertain. The current prevalence of short-format use indicates that the longer the audio or video content, the smaller the base of consumers who are willing to watch/listen to the entire program. Therefore, to reach the largest audience, business- and consumer-oriented companies should create content that is less than 15 minutes long. Longer content may be able to reach a large audience if it is broken into discrete, sub-15-minute segments that can easily be stopped, restarted, and skipped. However, given that the analysis neither asked respondents how long they are willing to use digital media nor correlated availability with usage, the issue needs further research before any strong conclusions can be drawn.

Live webcasts generally range between 1 and 2 hours in length for your typical product launch, press announcement, conference call, or company announcement. However, live webcasts can't be searched and indexed and therefore require a user to have to sit through the entire broadcast just to get a specific piece of information. In most cases, there is not much you can do when it comes to live broadcasts, but previous chapters suggest that you know what you want to feature, how to highlight it, and what clear message you want to deliver in the shortest period of time.

5.7 Encoding bit rates affect content quality—and your target audience

There are more choices than ever when it comes to encoding your audio and video assets. But before you decide on codecs, platforms, or distribution methods there are some things you need to think about which directly affect how many people can view your content and what the quality will be.

There are a number of things to think about before you start to encode. What is the content? The nature of the content will be a big deciding factor in the quality. Video content that has less motion and no quick pans, like a press conference of someone standing still behind a podium, is naturally going to look better than quick moving video of a sports event.

What has been edited? When thinking about how you present your content on the Web, realize that the typical viewer watches less than 5 minutes of video. Review your content and highlight the most important sections. What are the scenes you want to make sure your viewers see? Try to edit your content so that it can be viewed in small, manageable sections. If you put up 60 minutes of video and make viewers try to find the relevant sections, it is most likely that your message will be missed.

What is your source? When it comes to encoding, the quality of the original master source will be one of the biggest factors in the quality of the finished encoded file. Whenever possible, if encoding from an archive, always use the original. Encode content from an archived tape like a DigiBeta, Beta, or miniDV. This will result in better quality than if encoded from a VHS source.

Who are your end viewers? The ultimate reason for encoding your content for viewing on the Web is to allow for a broader and larger range of viewership. Knowing who your audience is allows you to make sure you are going to encode the content in the right format and bit rate. For instance, if you wanted to reach the widest possible audience on the Web you would need to select multiple bit rates that allow everyone, from dial-up users to broadband users, to access your content. While you may want to encode your content at only 300 Kbps because it looks best, remember that without high-speed access some viewers would not be able to watch your content.

Does it need to be live? When it comes to encoding your audio or video decide on whether your content needs to be encoded and streamed live, or can be captured and encoded for on-demand viewing. Encoding your content for a live stream adds additional cost to the project, unlike encoding it later from an archived format.

Encoding by itself is pretty simple for most applications. Encoding from a source is as easy as pointing to the source file or input, choosing a name for the destination file, picking audio/video codecs, choosing the bit rate, and clicking start. All of the major encoding software packages (RealProducer, Windows Media, QuickTime, Media Cleaner, etc.) have built-in wizard templates to make the job even easier. All you need to do is simply pick the template describing the target viewing audience and the codecs and bit rates are automatically defined. So even if you are new to the encoding process, the wizard templates in the software help make the process simple. With a little practice, you can compare the results obtained from the different wizard settings and you'll be up and encoding in no time.

5.8 Case Studies

5.8.1 Citigroup

Citigroup is the first financial services company in the United States to bring together banking, insurance, and investments under one umbrella. With the most diverse array of products and the greatest distribution capacity of any financial firm in the world, its 275,000 employees manage 200 million customer accounts across 6 continents in more than 100 countries.

Citigroup is not new to the concept of leveraging video within its organization. In fact, the company has been using video, such as one-way training videos to over 500 client branches worldwide, for over 8 years. Citigroup internally managed a world-class television studio for production of live broadcasts as well as videos that were used both internally and externally. However, this model had limitations. The company was constrained in its reach because the cost to produce live and on-demand video presentations was expensive, and maintaining tight control was a challenge. It became apparent that Citigroup needed a robust and cost-effective delivery infrastructure, but at the time the technology to accomplish this just didn't exist. However, with the advent of CDNs, that all changed.

Tony Raimundo, Senior Vice President, Digital Media Technology, had the task to build a new, cost-effective delivery infrastructure that could scale to support hundreds of thousands of users worldwide. But it wasn't as simple as just finding the right content delivery system. Raimundo also needed an application to interact with and monitor the network so that content could be safely delivered over the network to locations where it was needed. The application had to control which viewers could access selected media. It also had to enable the business users to publish content without relying on IT resources, while still maintaining overall IT control. After evaluating several different technologies, Raimundo and his team determined that an integrated solution with MPI's Media Publisher (www.media-publisher.com) application and the chosen Content Delivery Networking Solution was the only option that could provide Citigroup with the robust functionality that matched its requirements.

MPI recognized the need for an enterprise CDN to be tightly integrated with the management and publishing software application. Media Publisher was designed over 4 years ago to address just that issue. "MPI understood why we were building this streaming video infrastructure. We could articulate our requirements and they intrinsically got it and in the cases where the technology didn't exist yet, it was a part of their roadmap. We weren't asking them to build us a customized solution, we were going there together," said Raimundo. "We also had the same ideology on the concept of a business publisher, and were on the same page in terms of importance for the internal network and application system to be fully integrated."

When asked how Media Publisher differed from the other solutions Citigroup evaluated, Raimundo responded, "Media Publisher is a very, very robust software set with a mastery of the levers required to deliver the robust, comprehensive media publishing system that best meets the needs of Citigroup's video infrastructure. No other product was comparable in providing the depth and breadth of functionality we required."

The implementation of Media Publisher and the CDN went smoothly. In the coming months, Media Publisher and the CDN will be integrated with 400 Citigroup portals, such as GEO (Global Equities Online portal) and Citivision, with Media Publisher as the master control system. The geographic reach will be to 4,000–5,000 of its 6,000 global offices, reaching 150,000 PCs by the end of this year and adding another 150,000 during 2005.

One video infrastructure can serve many business functions. The video infrastructure is used for a variety of business cases, such as executive communications, live and on-demand training, and research. Of those three, it is most widely used with executive communications. Executives want to create a shared vision, and the best way to convey that message isn't with e-mail or presentations. With video communications, they can communicate using verbal and nonverbal cues; their audiences feel a sense of corporate culture with this form of communication delivery.

New executives want to put their imprint on business units. Some will get on a plane and travel around the world, but many of those trips can be supplemented with regular broadcasts. Prior to this technology rollout, when Citigroup executives wanted to communicate at a company-wide level, it was necessary to set up conference rooms with live feeds. Now, end users receive streamed content directly to their desktops.

Training throughout the branches is also enhanced. Instead of asking employees to watch DVDs or videotapes, live or on-demand training can be delivered straight to the employee's desktop. And rather than using the "honor system" for tracking completion, Media Publisher's built-in reporting tools combined with the CDN manager give up-to-the minute usage data, right down to the individual employee's viewing history.

This system can be easily adopted. By leveraging a digital media system, Citigroup now provides employees with a variety of technical and media skills so they can interact with video content. These include creative, video-savvy producers who don't want to change their current flow of doing things, as well as nontechnical business users. For example, if a business executive wants to talk to his bankers in the Middle East at 9:00 a.m., he no longer needs to request IT to make it happen. "Media Publisher automates the process from scheduling the encoders to pushing the streamed video over the network. IT resources no longer need to be called upon to manually set things up," said Raimundo. "People just show up and watch the event from any Internet connection."

Cost savings can be seen with this new system. Before this new infrastructure was in place, if a Citigroup business unit wanted to do a video broadcast to 50 companies, it could cost anywhere between $20,000 and 50,000 per event. Costs included studio time; IT resources; and creating and shipping tapes, CDs, or DVDs. Now with the video infrastructure in place, the cost is trivial. Citigroup will save hundreds of thousands of dollars per year overall.

In the financial world, timely information is crucial. A perfect example is the morning call, which ties up brokers and equity sales reps for the next 4–5 hours. If the information is delayed, even by an hour, the information is worthless. With the new video infrastructure in place, there is no lag time. The system is in place to deliver time-sensitive information the moment it is created. This feature is critical because customers count on Citigroup to provide them with the latest, most accurate information.

Increased customer value is seen with this solution. Some customers want to capture intellectual property and monetize it. At the moment, Citigroup is giving intellectual property to its high-end customers at no charge as a value-added service. "The reason why companies don't typically do this is because they cannot control the assets," said Raimundo. "However, with our new solution, Citigroup can create valuable content and control where it's distributed so it's only given to the intended audience. At the end of the day, we have happier customers."

This is just the beginning for Citigroup. With an effective enterprise video communications solution now in place, reaching both internal and external constituents, there are virtually endless possibilities for leveraging the new system to enhance Citigroup's services to their employees and customers. For more information on this case study visit www.media-publisher.com.

5.8.2 Marist College

Under its Shared University Research program, IBM introduced a collaborative effort with Marist College in New York to supply a combination of software, hardware, and services to enable a digital media infrastructure that supports the creation, storage, and exchange of digitized content using the Internet. The project was called Greystone and went live in September 2003 for the start of the fall semester. The key goals for Marist College and Project Greystone included:

- Understanding effective teaching and instructional design in e-learning
- Evaluating content management and course management systems to support e-learning
- Understanding cost structures and ROI for e-learning
- Providing "best of breed" systems and support for Marist faculty engaged in e-learning
- Providing content management and course management systems to internal and external constituencies using an e-utility or computing on-demand model
- Assuring that all e-learners become a part of the Marist community and develop a sense of loyalty to the college

Education is undergoing a technology-driven revolution. Digital storage and data mining, multimedia learning objects, the Web and the Internet, portals, and virtual communities are just some of the technologies that will form the future of teaching and learning. Marist, and other learning institutions, are being challenged to:

- Extend the reach of e-learning
- Provide rich-media learning content
- Manage and distribute rich media for existing digital collections
- Provide learning management and reporting
- Provide a common interface portal for all services

Project Greystone is a rich-media infrastructure designed to meet these challenges. Built on state-of-the-art technologies, Greystone combines IBM's world-class middleware, proven server and storage products, emerging Research & Development, and global services with Cisco's industry-leading distribution and caching solutions to produce an original modular media utility that can integrate with most third-party learning management systems (LMS).

This solution supports the creation, storage, and delivery of content, in the form of rich-media learning objects, to the end user. It includes a portal component to support virtual communities and end-user personalization, special router technology to enable class-based broadcasting, abstraction of digital media storage using XML cataloging, an enterprise content management system, IMS-based meta-tagging of learning objects, and caching devices to push content to the edge of the network. The solution architecture is explained in Figure 5.2.

The infrastructure is built around the digital media delivery solution developed by IBM and Cisco Systems. The solution enables enterprises to deliver digital media, which includes live video. This integrated solution is delivered in a stand-alone rack that includes the necessary hardware and software to create, distribute, and manage rich digital media information and services. The digital media delivery solution integrates the Cisco application and content networking system (ACNS) with the IBM DB2 content manager, IBM WebSphere portal server, and IBM's rich-media distribution utility to address the changing requirements of Marist's environment.

This infrastructure included the following components:

Delivering rich capabilities for education portal functionality— Security-rich log-in, portlets and tabbed workplaces, personalization, and customization.

Community tools—e-mail, instant messaging, presence awareness, discussion groups, administrative forms with workflow, teamroom environments, orientation packets, LMS for posting notes and assignments, professional development materials, and orientation modules for new faculty.

Multicast capability—A new approach to multicast that makes it practical to have a large number of small groups receive broadcast data from applications like voice over IP, collaboration, e-meetings, and more. It is well-suited to a school environment in which a large number of small groups, such as individual classes, require rich synchronous communication tools without flooding the network.

Content distribution network—Ideal for a physically distributed campus. Content can be pre-positioned or cached at the edge of the network, which

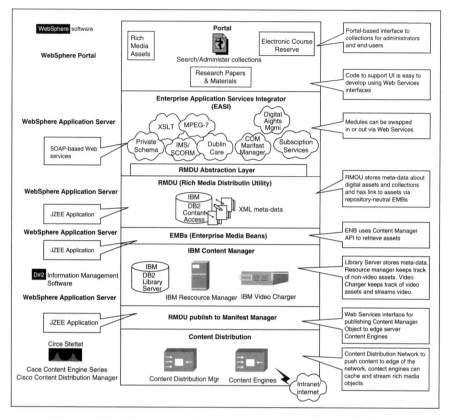

Figure 5.2: *Greystone solution architecture at Marist College.*

reduces traffic to the hosting center and helps improve performance and access to existing digital media assets. Live video can also be streamed from the edge of the network.

Digital media stack—An enterprise content management system with video streaming (including MPEG-1 and MPEG-2) capability to deliver rich-media assets. The XML metadata layer can describe any type of digital asset using IMS-compliant meta-tagging. A Web services interface allows integration with an existing LMS.

Streaming or Digital Media Project Management: How to Implement and Manage a Profitable Business

6.1 Based on interviews with people building these systems today, here are some guidelines for building and managing a streaming or digital media business

As discussed in previous chapters, today's market for streaming media products and services is mature enough to learn from past mistakes, success stories, and lessons learned from those who have been working with this technology for the past few years. With any industry there are always a select group of companies who are innovators that adopt and use new technology faster than others. But today, with streaming and digital media technologies becoming mainstream, the time has come where no company needs to stand by and wait for others to blaze the trail. The kinks have been worked out, the business models exist, and the technology is advanced enough for any company in any vertical to use it to their advantage.

With that in mind, here are some guidelines to be aware of when building and managing a streaming or digital media business. (These guidelines can also be found as a bullet list at the end of the chapter.) First, make sure there is buy-in from upper management and you have enough of a budget to accomplish at least a valid test of the technology and business. You don't need to start off with a large budget or large project, but if you don't have management buy-in on even a test case scenario, a larger scale deployment will be difficult. How do I get upper management buy-in and how do I show the value for the dollars they will spend? That is a valid question and one you have to answer to prove what you are doing adds value to the bottom line. Remember, for most people streaming media is not their core business, so think of the technology in terms of other commodity services. How do you show value by having a telephone, fax, Web site, and e-mail? Streaming and digital media systems are no different. Decide what your need for streaming media is, devise a way to show how it is judged to be successful, and use that to guide your long-term strategy and short-term buy-in from management.

When devising your project, make sure to plan expenditures and project time lines in phases. I've seen many examples of companies who have a good plan going into the project but try to do way too much in a very short time frame. If done properly over time, the value streaming media holds for an organization grows steadily over time. Don't feel the need to have to try to accomplish everything in one month. Roll it out in phases that gradually involve more technology to a wider audience with more use and continue to measure the impact it has on your business over that time.

As mentioned before, have a means to track and evaluate the ROI from the implemented systems and technology. Also, ask yourself how streaming media has allowed you to reach a wider audience, communicate more effectively, reduce expenses and overhead, create a larger margin on sales, establish a better brand, etc. It is essential to know these things as well as the many ways one can benefit from the technology. First, do a search in your vertical for companies who have already used this technology in your industry and read about the ways they have benefited. Find out how your competition is using streaming and digital media technology by visiting their Web site and also by going to www.streamingmedia.com and searching on keywords involved in your project. So if you want to do a webcast and are in the financial sector, doing a search on www.streamingmedia.com for "financial webcasting" will bring up articles and press releases of what others are doing and have announced in the industry. This is a great way to educate yourself very quickly about what is taking place in the market. Keep in mind not to allow yourself to get overwhelmed with all the available technology and stay focused on the ROI from the technology and applications you read about.

Since we are on the subject of ROI, you should also plan multiple business applications with the streaming media technology to showcase the varied scale of ROI for the application used. For example, if you are doing a trial with a webcast project internally, make sure to use it in a corporate communications application such as an external CEO broadcast as well as an internal marketing or human resources training function. When used in various applications to solve various needs, you will find that your organization may determine a higher ROI for a specific vertical, be it internal or external. Doing this will also expose you and your company to a wider role for the planned technology and may allow you to come across a new way to use it.

Since you are reading this book you are probably already aware that no matter what project you implement, having your IT department, group, or person involved or at least educated on what you are doing is a smart move on your part. For some projects, those where you are building a streaming media system for deployment with an organization, or for one where you need those in your organization to access the content, the IT group will play a large part in your success, whether you like it or not. With most people, there are usually two sides to the story when it comes to the IT department. Some are worried that if they involve the IT department they will get too much push back because the IT department may not be aware of today's technology and the real impact it may have on the corporate network. Without the IT department, especially in a large organization, you aren't going to be able to deliver this content to employees internally, even if you are delivering it from an outside CDN. The IT department usually pushes back on technology not because it is worried or scared to use it, but because they are brought in at the last minute and not kept in the loop. With the help of the IT department you will be able to determine if everyone in your organization has the right media player on their desktop, has a sound and video card, and some external speakers, but above all else they have the ability to have open ports on the firewall to allow streaming onto the network. The IT department is also the front line support for you if end users have any problems, and they can also be your biggest help in getting this all done quickly. Not involving the IT department and having them complain later on to management will not help you accomplish your goal and will only make it harder to get management buy-in. If everyone is on the same page and agrees on what needs to be done and how to accomplish it, the project tends to go smoother. With that said, sometimes you may need to fight to show IT that this isn't as hard as they make it out to be and that the IT department doesn't need to do it all internally. Some IT departments think they need to do everything in-house and that outsourcing any technology aspect makes them look like failures. However, this is not the case. Outsourcing is an acceptable practice to meet your telecommunications needs, so outsourcing your media tapes to get encoded is also considered acceptable and not as a failure of the IT department.

At some point you need to do a cost comparison of outsourcing versus doing some aspect or all aspects of your project in-house. One of the things to remember when first adopting streaming media and testing the waters is that you can do it inexpensively by using an outside CDN or service provider, which will give you the ability to get your feet wet and experience what is available on the market today. This will help you get a first-hand look at the technology, the applications it is used for, and the ways it can be deployed without having to spend a lot of money. Later in this chapter we'll discuss how to research and decide whether to build up an internal infrastructure or use an external CDN.

6.2 Pricing: understanding costs and what you should pay

For all of the advances in the streaming media industry over the years—from improved compression technology, the introduction of additional hardware devices, and the different business models emerging—the most commonly asked and confusing question corporations still face is how to pick the right service provider and what they should pay for their services. The following section provides an overview of what you need to know in order to choose the right service provider with the most reliable and cost-effective solution for your needs.

6.2.1 The service provider business

Since the introduction of service providers, the models by which their services are marketed, priced, and delivered have changed faster than any other aspect of the business. Choosing the right service provider still continues to be a difficult task. You must first cut through all the marketing hype, opinions, and confusing product pitches. Outsourcing all or part of the process can leave you with more questions than answers.

The basics—So let's start at the beginning. What are service providers and what services do they really offer? The term service provider is pretty generic these days. Service providers come in many forms and sizes and can provide many pieces of the total solution or specialize in just one aspect of the streaming media process. For example, some service providers may focus on just the encoding process or just the hosting aspect. Other service providers will offer many parts of the process, and almost every service provider works with partners to attempt to offer every possible solution you may require.

How the service provider business has evolved—Over the past 24 months the service provider space has drastically shrunk and consolidated. Many providers whose business models consisted of charging below cost for services just to gain market share have gone out of business or have been acquired by other providers. At last count, there are over 35 providers who have been acquired or closed their doors in the past 24 months. As this sector of the industry has changed, many providers have adjusted their business models and are now focused on what should always have been their primary concern—profit and loss. Because of this, many of the pricing models continue to evolve making it difficult for corporations to distinguish prices and services from one provider to another.

Why the confusion?—One of the most confusing things about most service providers is that they don't explain their services in layman's terms. Many service providers seem to think that if they keep this technology confusing and make it sound more complicated than it is, customers will be willing to stay uneducated and trust what they say. What they don't understand is that the more they educate the customer and show them the value of the technology and a viable way to measure their ROI, the more the client will utilize their services. Not all service providers deal with clients this way, but many still do and the model by which they sell these services is changing every day. It was less than only 48 months ago that clients thought they needed tens of thousands of streams when it came to live webcasting, yet now clients have been educated to the point that their expectations are becoming more realistic. This is due to clients educating themselves and taking the time to understand the advantages these applications offer.

6.2.2 Educating yourself before you talk to providers

When should you decide to use service providers for your streaming media needs and what should you be aware of?

Cut through the hype—Once you have decided to go with a service provider for some or all of your rich-media needs, there is some basic information you should know both from a business side as well as a product side of the equation. First, realize that the majority of the provider's pitch is marketing hype. Providers need to realize that this is *not* about the technology or the products they are offering. The technology and products mean nothing unless they are the solution to a problem. It is not about the newest or greatest technology but rather the solutions that move your business forward. Many providers have different names for their products and services, but initially the service is the same.

The biggest myth—Probably the biggest myth when it comes to service providers is who offers the best "quality." Many providers talk about how they offer the best encoding or hosting quality, yet there are very few ways to judge their technical quality. Additionally, there is no third-party organization providing unbiased, reliable data that compares providers from the same technical perspective. When talking about quality remember that the quality of the service is not always based on one factor, but a variety of factors such as ease of use, price, scalability, and customer service. As with anything you purchase, the quality of that purchase should be judged on many variables.

It's not about the technology or products—Don't get caught up in the technology and products of providers. Each service provider markets and sells its products and services differently, and the key thing to remember is that the technology and products they are using mean nothing unless it solves your problem. Most providers use words like "mission-critical," "top-tier," and "cutting-edge" when describing their products. However, if these products don't address the needs of your particular problem, then it doesn't matter how cutting-edge their technology is.

6.2.3 Choosing the right provider is easy

The easiest way to pick the right provider is like shopping for a car. Get multiple quotes and solution pitches so you have a good understanding of the different options available. Educate yourself on the background of the company and their service offering. Choosing the right provider is easy if you follow these guidelines and keep in mind the points listed below before you sign a contract.

Don't get into the format wars—Don't get caught up in the choice of content distribution format. Choosing the type of streaming media format is actually the easiest part of the equation. Service providers have an excellent understanding of the pros and cons of each streaming media format and can advise you as to which one they feel would suit you best based on your goals. Additionally, when it comes to distributing your content, most providers don't charge you extra to distribute one type of format over another, so many times it is economical to be able to deliver your content in multiple formats.

It's all about setting correct expectations—Always go with a provider that takes the time to educate you and listen to your needs. If the provider isn't willing to educate you before you sign a contract, how much do you think they are going to educate you *after* they already have you locked into a contract? No matter how good a deal seems or how reputable the service provider is, if they don't educate you and set your expectations properly and follow up on those expectations, they are not the service provider for you.

Contract rules—Don't get pressured into signing a multi-year deal. Pricing for streaming media services only continues to get cheaper as time goes on, so don't let the providers scare you into thinking you have to sign a multi-year deal for their services to be economical. Also, by signing a shorter contract, you are able to change service providers without having to pay early termination fees to get out of a contract.

Get first-hand advice—The most important advice when choosing the right provider is to get recommendations from others who use them. Find out what they have liked and disliked about the provider. Most providers will also let you test their services for a trial period, which allows hands-on time with their products and tools. Any provider that is unwilling to let you test their "packaged" services is not really interested in winning your business.

6.2.4 The going rate

The wide range of pricing among providers doesn't make it any easier for customers looking to outsource some aspect of streaming media. One provider may be charging $5,000 for a live webcast, but another provider who appears to be providing the exact same service might be charging $15,000. Commodities like megabyte transferred, which starts at about $4 a gigabyte or $0.004 per megabyte and goes down to $0.80 per gigabyte or $0.0008 per megabyte for a 10 TB + commitment, or storage, which starts at about $20 a gigabyte and goes down to $5 a gigabyte in volume, seem comparable. Streaming media prices for applications, professional services, encoding, etc., are all over the map.

To answer questions about how pricing works, why it changes, and how to best to get a handle on it, StreamingMedia.com released a second edition of the report *The Cost of Streaming Services*. This report is an analysis of service provider pricing on the market and what the going industry rate is for services. (A full copy of the report can be acquired at www.streamingmedia.com/research.)

The Cost of Streaming Services has revealed the following list of principal truths:

1. Service prices from the top providers have been extremely stable for the past 12 months. Three of the top six streaming services providers have not changed their service prices for the past 12 months.

2. New providers are undercutting established service prices. Streaming service providers that started operations within the past 18 months offer streaming services at rates that deeply undercut the rates of the established service providers, roughly by a factor of 3 to 5.

3. There has been a significant consolidation among leading service providers. Three companies that were among the leading service providers years ago no longer offer such services (Intel Media Services, iBeam, and Cable & Wireless). One other top provider has chosen to entirely move away from basic streaming services and re-focus toward high-end consulting and production services. Thus, almost half of 2003's top ten service providers are no longer serving this market.

4. Industry-wide pricing will remain stable until leading providers are forced to move. Our conclusion is that leading service providers won't significantly drop their service prices until forced to do so by lower priced streaming services or do-it-yourselfers.

5. Service prices vary widely. Most providers price services according to the following rules:

   • Leading service providers price on-demand streaming from a high of roughly $0.01 per megabyte to a fraction of a penny per megabyte, as guaranteed monthly volume of transfer increases from zero to several terabytes (millions of megabytes). On-demand streaming prices from newer providers range from $0.01 down to one-quarter of a cent at terabyte volumes.

   • Live streaming prices range from $20 per stream-hour to $0.20 per stream-hour, as the guaranteed number of simultaneous streams and event duration increase.

   • Encoding prices range from $20 per minute down to $1 per minute.

   • Storage costs are more narrowly contained, varying from roughly $0.20 cents per megabyte to $0.04 cents, as storage volume increases from just above zero to hundreds of gigabytes.

   • Consulting prices range from $100 to more than $400 per hour.

5. To determine what pricing to expect from the best service providers, see Appendix A: Guide to Rates. You'll be able to find your scenario(s) in a simple set of tables, and see the pricing that's common for each scenario with monthly and yearly budgets. You can also find some helpful advice on how to choose your service provider(s). Although prices have varied widely while some key streaming services have changed in the past year, price variation between vendors has not. Likewise, the reason for this variation remains the same: The streaming industry faces an extremely challenging marketplace. Not only does the streaming industry ride the volatile dot-com roller coaster along with most other public and privately

held Internet and technology companies, but it has also seen its own significant changes of focus and business models.

6. Countless new media companies have risen and failed within the last year and a half, which has caused significant negative pressure on investment in new media companies.

7. Although substantial broadband deployment continues today, much of the streaming industry has turned its primary focus toward enterprise use of streaming. This change of focus away from consumers and toward business (from B2C to B2B) may fundamentally alter the underlying business models of service providers.

8. The streaming industry is still relatively young, and prices simply have not yet had time to stabilize. Most service providers didn't even exist five years ago. These companies are pioneering new business models.

The complexity of serving a wide array of customers, from small content streamers to corporate enterprise networks, makes it challenging to devise a suitable pricing policy. It also makes it quite difficult for service providers to stabilize their own business models and prices. This is one of the main factors that compelled us to undertake this research effort. It is our primary goal to help the streaming industry by publishing the current state of pricing in a rapidly changing environment. By doing this we hope to help both service providers and their customers create and refine robust business models for their streaming efforts.

The best way to ensure that you are not overpaying for your streaming services is to negotiate with several service providers. To give you some leverage in negotiations, we've created a suite of representative scenarios, based mainly on the leading service provider rate cards, with associated "fair" pricing. This serves as an outline of what other streamers in your situation are paying. To calculate your streaming budget find a scenario in one of the tables below that matches yours, and you'll see the mid-range price offered by providers. Table 6.1 covers on-demand streaming, and Table 6.2 covers live streaming. Your costs should largely be determined by these factors:

- How many megabytes you stream monthly (for on-demand streaming)
- The number of simultaneous viewers you expect, and the duration of live events
- Whether you are located in the United States or elsewhere

If you were to compare the data with the same table of data from 2002, you would see that the biggest budget changes will occur among the lowest volume streamers. Thus, if your monthly streaming volume is 250,000 MB or more, your on-demand streaming budget will be virtually unchanged from a year ago. For volumes below that, there has been a dramatic decline in costs, from a high of $0.10 per megabyte (as reported in the first edition) to just $0.03 per megabyte. This decline in entry-level streaming costs is a direct reflection of the rate-card reduction among leading service providers to align themselves with the rate structures of the other leading providers.

Although four of the top five service providers have not changed their live event pricing from last year, the budget cited in Table 6.2 is significantly lower than the live event budget that was published in last year's edition of this report. There is a simple reason for this: Last year's budget was based entirely on the rates of one of the top two providers, whose rates are no longer representative of the other four top providers now included in our data. Last year, we cautiously calculated the live event budgets by using a top provider that, although not the low-price leader, was so well established and so widely used that its price structure was a good conservative choice for what the reader could expect. Now that the other four leading providers all have prices that are lower (at the low end of audience size and stream duration), the reader has an excellent opportunity to obtain live event pricing in this lower range (as shown in Figure 6.2). Probably the hardest part of budgeting your streaming costs is forecasting the amount of content that you expect to stream. The best forecasts are based on actual previous experience, everything else is total guesswork. In the second half of 2005, StreamingMedia.com will publish its "Cost of Streaming Services, 3rd Edition" Research Report.

6.2.5 Our best advice: negotiate

The best way to ensure that you're not overpaying for your streaming services is to negotiate with several major service providers. Using the tables in this report, it is easy to determine just how much other streamers in your situation are paying for the same services. Considering the structures of provider rate cards we have obtained, "fair-market" streaming costs should be directly determined by the following criteria:

- How much total streaming you do (whether this is measured by megabytes, stream-hours, or bandwidth): Leading service providers don't always charge huge monthly fees or high per-unit charges; there are often volume discounts.
- Where you are located: Geography matters when it comes to bandwidth costs. The United States has the lowest bandwidth costs, while South America and Asia have the highest, according to our data. There isn't much you can do about this, as even moving your servers to the United States would bring added costs and quality considerations.

- Whether you value premium services such as content delivery, consulting, etc.
- Your industry sector—and, to a lesser degree, the size of your company—can also affect how much you can expect to pay.

6.2.6 Quality—getting your money's worth

In the end, price is usually not the paramount consideration in the selection of streaming service providers. In fact, more often than not, it's stream quality, depth and breadth of service, reliability, and other criteria that matter more. That's because everyone—the audience, the content owner, the service provider, and the ISP—is unhappy when content is served with poor quality. But it's very hard to determine how well or poorly any of your content is being streamed. Sometimes the only sign of a problem is a significant drop in viewers, and streaming quality may not even be the problem (sometimes it may be the content itself that's limiting your audience). It can be difficult to determine what and who is responsible for poor streaming quality; it may be the encoding, the server, the provider network, the media player, or the Internet provider for the audience. There is a dearth of information, which is why there is a need for comprehensive reporting and insightful analysis of the reports. Trends in re-buffering, percentage of lost packets, and audience problem reports can be found, but how can the streaming quality of various service providers be compared? The problem is simply that there is no information available that objectively analyzes the quality of streaming and support services, and you have little more than the word of the service providers for the quality of their services.

6.3 Build versus buy

As mentioned earlier, at some point it may make sense for you to begin to evaluate the cost of doing some or all of your streaming media project internally versus outsourcing to a service provider. If you are a small organization, this decision is easy as you probably won't have the resources to take on such a project. For companies who have IT departments and an internal network, the cost savings over time from keeping the project in-house can add up.

Naturally, service providers are happy to pocket any additional margin they can capture from declining bandwidth prices while charging you to use their network without passing on that cost savings. But there is a limit to just how far this can go before providers start losing business to do-it-yourselfers.

This happens because at some price point, the price incentive to do it yourself is just too good to ignore. Despite the technical challenges and costs of hardware, software, maintenance, and implementation involved, many Fortune 1000 companies are looking at alternative means to cache, store, and distribute their content or are already doing it themselves. This change depends on the company and its infrastructure and financial situation, among other factors. For example, if your company could lease employee PCs for just $1 a month, you'd never buy another PC, but if leasing costs $100 a month, PC purchase becomes the more sensible and economically attractive alternative. Unfortunately companies often make build/buy decisions based on a multitude of factors, not just cost. So as streamers consider the possibility of doing it themselves, there are several factors that are usually far more important than price, most notably, quality and control.

6.3.1 Quality

If you control your own network, you can fully control the streaming quality of the content you distribute, but you will never have this control when you outsource to a service provider. Although all bandwidth providers offer service level agreements (SLAs) that guarantee quality of service (QOS) for the bandwidth delivered, no streaming provider offers similar guarantees for streaming delivery services. Several CDNs offer edge caching versus centralized storage, but they don't guarantee streaming QOS, because they are unable to do so for streaming on the open Internet. Thus, whether or not you're getting what you're paying for remains an unresolved question.

6.3.2 Control

Whenever you outsource, the responsibility and authority for ensuring stream quality and security belong to the service provider. This may not be acceptable to some streamers (for highly classified material and/or for material that must be delivered with the highest video quality). The right mix for your company largely depends on which streaming projects you deploy. For some companies, especially in the current economy, cost savings will be paramount and price will often be the dominant factor in the decision. For other companies, the viewable quality of the content may be even more important than cost. For instance, people won't pay $5 for an online movie that repeatedly stops and re-buffers and has unacceptably low audio/video quality. Many medical applications, such as remote surgery, will also require highly reliable and sustained video quality as well as extremely low latency. For others, considerations of access and control may predominate. The only sensible approach is to examine and evaluate all of these factors in order to determine the right mix of "build" and "buy" for your situation. There is no one solution that fits every need.

6.4 Understanding the most commonly used multimedia applications for enterprise communications

When it comes to deciding on what applications you are going to manage, having a grasp of the most common applications for enterprise communication can help you to design your plan. Exactly half of the 1,206 corporate executives surveyed by Interactive Media Strategies (IMS) in the fourth quarter of 2003 said that their company deployed webcasts that year. The penetration of audio- and video-enriched applications grew in 2004 as 93 percent of all survey respondents report plans to keep webcasting budgets in 2004 at or above their 2003 levels.

Employee training and executive presentations continue to top the list of most popular multimedia applications among companies that have deployed webcasting (Figure 6.1). Sixty-one percent of all firms that use webcasting have deployed these two specific uses for the technology. These penetration levels represent significant growth in the penetration of these applications. In a fourth quarter 2002 IMS survey, deployment levels for employee training and executive presentations stood at 47 and 40 percent, respectively.

Large companies—firms with more than 2,500 employees—continue to dominate the landscape of webcast deployment. Of all the companies producing more than 50 webcasts annually, 73 percent are organizations with more than 2,500 workers. However, survey responses hint that Web-based multimedia communications stand on the cusp of moving into the corporate mainstream. Companies that historically have allocated mid-sized budgets for webcasting (between $10,000 and $100,000 a year) are showing greater interest than any other group in deploying new webcasting technology.

Video-enhanced applications appear to be garnering more interest from would-be webcast spenders than those applications integrating only audio. Already, survey respondents report deployment levels for video applications that outstrip comparable uses of audio. The gap in video and audio deployment is poised to grow as more corporate executives initiate webcasting applications that incorporate video components.

Table A.1 *Budgeting your On-Demand Streaming Costs*

Monthly Volume of Streaming (MBs)	U.S. or ROW	Cents per MB	Monthly Budget	Yearly Budget
10,000	United States	3.0	$300	$3,600
50,000	United States	3.0	$1,500	$18,000
100,000	United States	2.5	$2,500	$30,000
250,000	United States	2.0	$5,000	$60,000
500,000	United States	1.8	$9,000	$108,000
1,000,000	United States	1.5	$15,000	$180,000
5,000,000	United States	0.9	$45,000	$540,000
10,000,000	United States	0.8	$80,000	$960,000
10,000	Rest of World	4.2	$420	$5,040
50,000	Rest of World	4.2	$2,100	$25,200
100,000	Rest of World	3.5	$3,500	$42,000
250,000	Rest of World	2.8	$7,000	$84,000
500,000	Rest of World	2.5	$12,500	$150,000
1,000,000	Rest of World	2.1	$21,000	$252,000
5,000,000	Rest of World	1.1	$55,000	$660,000
10,000,000	Rest of World	1.0	$100,000	$1,200,000

Figure 6.1

In this report, IMS provides an overview of webcast deployment trends in the corporate sector. This report summarizes the general characteristics of the companies that have invested in the deployment of webcasting in the past year and identifies how the characteristics of companies using multimedia are changing. The second half of the report discusses deployment trends for different webcasting applications and assesses the influence of video and audio on multimedia deployment patterns during the application. More information from this report is available at www.interactivemediastrategies.com.

6.5 A summary checklist to use when building a successful streaming business

Refer to this checklist when building your streaming and digital media business:

1. Make sure there is buy-in from upper management with a satisfactory budget.

2. Plan expenditures and architecture landscape in phases.
3. Determine a means to establish ROI.
4. Plan multiple business applications for higher ROI—such as corporate communications, training, human resources, financial, product demos, marketing, etc.
5. Develop a strong relationship with the IT group.
6. Research and decide whether to build up internal infrastructure or use an external CDN.
7. Decide what streaming format and version to use, one preferably to keep costs and post-production time down.
8. Determine and assign project roles and responsibilities.

6.6 Case studies

6.6.1 The Cooper Companies

Corporate annual meetings are key focal points on the corporate financial calendar that give investors direct access to a company's senior management. It is an opportunity for shareholders to review corporate policies, performance, and plans. This is particularly important at this time of heightened interest in corporate governance. However, investor attendance can be a challenge as time constraints and travel logistics often prevent them from physically attending these important meetings. Many investors already remotely participate in annual meetings via proxy vote or conference calls, but while these options have undoubtedly helped, remote attendees are still at a disadvantage because interaction is so constrained.

The Cooper Companies (NYSE: COO), a rapidly growing specialty healthcare company whose business units serve attractive niche markets in the medical device market, recognized these issues and decided to supplement their physical annual meetings with a webcast in an effort to broaden shareholder participation in meetings. They turned to CCBN, a Boston-based webcasting communications company, to provide the virtual meetings to increase outreach to the investment community.

"Holding our annual meetings as webcasts as well as physical meetings allows shareholders to attend the meetings without incurring travel costs and that has greatly boosted investor participation," says Christie Bender, investor relations (IR) administrator at The Cooper Companies. "Participation in this year's webcast generated a 500 percent increase in attendance over our first webcast in 2000. What's more, the archive of the event attracted nearly twice that figure."

Table A.2 *Budgeting Your Live Streaming Costs*

	If You Stream Live Events:			Then You Can Expect to Pay:	
Audio/Video	Average Streaming Duration (hours)	# Simultaneous Streams	U.S. or ROW	$ for Each Simultaneous Stream Hour	Budget per Event
audio	1.00	100	United States	$1.50	$150
audio	1.00	500	United States	$.60	$300
audio	1.00	1,000	United States	$.50	$500
audio	2.00	100	United States	$.75	$150
audio	2.00	500	United States	$.30	$300
audio	2.00	1,000	United States	$.25	$500
video	1.00	100	United States	$15.63	$1,563
video	1.00	500	United States	$6.25	$3,125
video	1.00	1,000	United States	$5.21	$5,208
video	2.00	100	United States	$7.81	$1,563
video	2.00	500	United States	$3.13	$3,125
video	2.00	1,000	United States	$2.60	$5,208
audio	1.00	100	Rest of World	$2.10	$210
audio	1.00	500	Rest of World	$.84	$420
audio	1.00	1,000	Rest of World	$.70	$700
audio	2.00	100	Rest of World	$1.05	$210
audio	2.00	500	Rest of World	$.42	$420
audio	2.00	1,000	Rest of World	$.35	$700
video	1.00	100	Rest of World	$21.88	$2,188
video	1.00	500	Rest of World	$8.75	$4,375
video	1.00	1,000	Rest of World	$7.29	$7,292
video	2.00	100	Rest of World	$10.94	$2,188
video	2.00	500	Rest of World	$4.38	$4,375
video	2.00	1,000	Rest of World	$3.65	$7,292

Figure 6.2

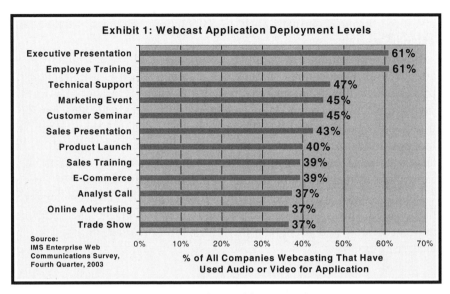

Figure 6.3

Many companies such as The Cooper Companies are choosing to offer virtual meetings to increase the efficiency of their financial communications with shareholders and potential shareholders. Interested parties are able to follow presentation slides in real time, gain a more in-depth grasp of the company's vision, and improve both their clarity of understanding and confidence in the management team. Analysts are also appreciating the initiative because they can now utilize the archive facility and extract information at will.

In addition to the improved access for those shareholders unable to travel to meetings, virtual webcasts save time and money for internal IR departments as they produce less paper, reduce mailing costs, generate fewer requests from shareholders for supporting materials, and reduce teleconference and replay costs. "It's been such a timesaver to have the presentation slides freely available to attendees via the webcast and later at the archive site rather than our department having to constantly respond to analysts' requests for the presentation slides," Bender notes. "Analysts are going back to the archive for information and as a result we're getting far fewer routine calls and e-mails for presentation material. That means we can devote our time and efforts to more strategic investment efforts." Outreach to the financial world is further enhanced with the use of CCBN's (www.ccbn.com) StreetEvents[SM] service—a network of over 15,000 institutional analysts and portfolio managers plus access to thousands of additional institutional investors through partners such as Bloomberg, Reuters, FactSet, and TheMarkets.com.

Before webcasting, The Cooper Companies had to individually alert attendees of an upcoming shareholder meeting, which is a time-intensive process. Now this is automated through the clients extranet, *My* CCBN, saving time and accommodating additional attendees who may not have traditionally been targeted. Following a webcast meeting the presentation link is posted to the StreetEvents service, which ensures outreach to the largest possible online investment community. Furthermore, the tracking capabilities available with the CCBN webcasting platform allow The Cooper Companies to see who's watching the webcast and when and how long they participated. This is valuable information to help them target their audience more accurately and strengthen the information provided to investors and analysts.

6.6.2 Office Depot, Inc.

Companies that support the communities in which they do business and build a reputation for strong corporate social responsibility are the ones most likely to grow and successfully expand their businesses. However, community outreach can pose significant issues for business. During the late 1990s, Office Depot, Inc., aggressively leveraged the Internet and B2B electronic commerce to establish itself as one of the industry's technology leaders. It also laid the seed for an innovative and far-reaching initiative that not only leveraged Office Depot's "What you Need, What you Need to Know" proposition, but it also established itself as a strong corporate supporter of small businesses and women's organizations. That initiative was the Office Depot Web Café, a dynamic and far-reaching communication tool that extended the company's contact with all prospective and current customers.

The company turned to CCBN, a Boston-based webcasting communications company, to develop and fine-tune this new interactive community and educational tool. CCBN had already built a strong partnership with Office Depot through its coordination of Office Depot's quarterly earnings webcasts.

Through its webcasts, Office Depot Web Café offers free seminars that focus on the changing business needs in the marketplace. In February, the Web Café was broadcast live from the Office Depot Success Strategies for Businesswomen Conference in Boca Raton, which offered programs and seminars to help women manage their businesses more successfully. This followed a season of hour-long webcasts from leading small business experts on topics including building a business, leaving a legacy, and maximizing technology.

The Office Depot Web Café offers virtual attendees the opportunity to enjoy a live video or audio presentation and the ability to participate in online question and answer sessions. Also, if you missed the live broadcast, the webcast can still be reviewed as an archive on the Office Depot Web site.

As Monica Luechtefeld, EVP of Global E-Commerce at Office Depot, explained, "The webcasts have consistently improved as we have added additional features to respond to the popularity of Web Café. We've had a lot of great feedback from the public with comments such as 'Great Idea' and 'Carry On'." A growing initiative, Office Depot looks forward to working with the webcasting application to help expand upon the current capabilities offered to Web Café attendees and allow Office Depot to better track customer satisfaction.

The next series of the Office Depot Web Café webcasts will address innovative ideas from leading business experts. This use of streaming media technology has allowed Office Depot to redefine customer communications in the office products sector and take e-commerce solutions to the next level of growth and success.

CHAPTER 7

Beyond Streaming Media: What Streaming and Digital Media Means to Other Areas of a Media Business

7.1 The Internet can significantly impact other areas of a media business

Every corporation knows the value of the Internet in its success. From e-mail, Web sites, and online ordering to inventory tracking, customer relationship management, and fulfillment, the Internet has quickly established itself as a tool that allows you to work smarter, more efficiently, and on a global scale. Streaming and digital media technology and applications are no different.

As you have read in previous chapters, the successful implementation of a streaming or digital media infrastructure can and should have a positive direct impact on the rest of your business. If it didn't do this, then what would its value be? For companies whose core focus is content or delivering entertainment, the digital media life cycle gives them the means and opportunity for creating new revenue-generating business models from their content. Streaming and digital media technologies allow industrial, financial, governmental, and traditional Fortune 500 enterprise non-media companies to empower, educate, and inform customers, employees, and shareholders. The use of streaming in most cases is not a replacement for other technology or applications, but rather complementary to them. The fax machine did not replace the phone as a business communication tool in the same way video streaming isn't replacing point-to-point video conferencing. They all work with one another and now we are finally beginning to see the different technologies work *with* one another. In the past, buying a product on the Internet was accomplished with a static click with no real interactive call to purchase. Today, for example, you can look at a video clip of a Black & Decker tool in action on their Web site before you buy. After purchase, you can receive training clips on how to use the tool, what attachments are made for it, and how to take care of it. Streaming media technology is now applied in real-world cases, in every industry and every vertical with great success.

As with any new technology, in the beginning people focus on the technology itself instead of its value. I am often asked: If this is the case, why do so many people still have questions on how streaming media works and how to use it? My answer to them each time is the same—it's a learning curve. It takes times for any technology or application to evolve from a stand-alone service to a seamless application. I know people who have e-mail, but don't know how to send an attachment or people who use a Web browser, but have no idea how to do searches for relevant content. Streaming and digital media are no different.

In 1997, a company called N2K (Need 2 Know) was one of the first to sell music singles on the Web for $0.99. At that time, this technology was revolutionary. N2K believed that people would want to buy songs online in a digital form and set out to prove it. They didn't succeed because at the time people were more focused on the technology than the application.

Little did anyone know that between 2003 and 2004 Apple Computer would sell 100 million songs via its online iTunes music store. Not only did selling songs online become a reality, but people quickly realized it was about the iTunes application and its ease of use, not about the iTunes technology. If you ask a consumer what they think of the iTunes service, they will talk about how easy it is to use, how cheap it is, and how convenient it is to buy music now. Rarely do they talk about the encoding, compression, storage, management, or tracking of the content.

This technology has now become mainstream, and with music, it is only just beginning. For Apple, the iTunes store is not about selling music, it's about selling hundreds of thousands of iPod media players that play the iTunes. Apple has publicly stated it does not make a profit on the iTunes store, it's the iPod hardware they make money on. Apple is a hardware company, but the Internet and digital media have had a direct impact on helping their core business.

7.2 Managed delivery: cut weeks out of media production cycles and push post-production times to the limit

One advantage to using digital media systems is the ability to shorten the time frame needed to create, edit, and publish content either internally or externally within an organization. The managed delivery component of a digital media system allows the content to get to market quicker, faster, and cheaper than other means of creation and distribution. We have all heard of independent filmmakers shooting and editing their film in a shorter time frame with available hardware and applications like Apple's Final Cut Pro. In some cases, filmmakers who would have spent 12 months shooting and editing a full-length movie have been able to reduce that production cycle down to half or even a quarter of that time. The same advantages apply to those who aren't in the media and entertainment verticals yet want to harness the power of these solutions to reduce the time and resources needed to create and deliver compelling content.

One example is a corporate communications presentation. Traditionally, a lot of time would be spent creating stand-alone elements such as audio, video, slides, and the Web interface. Then more time would be spent piecing these elements together. With the digital media solutions available, these tasks can be accomplished all at once in near-real time. After all, using today's technology to help communicate more efficiently and more effectively in a time-saving manner is a goal corporations are striving to achieve.

For many people, the old standby continues to be the PowerPoint presentations. Although these presentations are informative in nature, they don't allow the same kind of interaction and viewer retention that results from adding video. For most executives already familiar with creating PowerPoint presentations, the thought of adding interactive video components seems like a daunting task. However, adding video and interactive elements is a simple process that doesn't require a lot of post-production time thanks to the digital media tools and applications available today.

The process of adding the video component is quite simple. Along with your slide component, you need to have a way to capture your audio and video and be able to synchronize your slides with it. Because the majority of these types of presentations are talking head presentations, you can get good quality video with just a webcam. There are many webcams that can be used. If you already have a digital video camera, it can easily be re-purposed for capturing the video as well. The same holds true for audio. Simple clip-on microphones that plug into the computer will do the necessary audio capture. Once the video and audio is captured to your computer, putting it all together with the slides is a simple process when using some of the available software packages.

One of the best products on the market today in terms of functionality, ease of use, and price is made by Serious Magic (www.seriousmagic.com). Their product, Visual Communicator, has two versions, one for $199 that is suitable for Web-only based presentations and one for $399 that allows higher quality presentations to be produced for DVDs or CD-ROMs. One of the best features of Serious Magic products is that the software ships with a clip-on microphone, which enables you to capture a quality audio signal. A green screen background is also included so custom backgrounds can be added from their software template. Their software allows you to synchronize your slides and video, add subtitles, and create custom-branded interfaces simply by clicking some buttons. With their product, you can capture and create a video-based presentation within minutes without having to have any technical background or programming experience and without having to do post-production on your presentation. If you can plug a webcam into your computer and talk into a microphone, you can easily deliver your message in a professional looking manner. Just imagine the post-production time and resources that would be needed if you were to do this the traditional way. Today's applications help you cut content creation time in half.

Another favorite software application used by many companies is Microsoft Producer. This application, a free download from Microsoft (www.microsoft.com/producer), allows more online collaboration and includes more features in the production templates. This popular add-on for Microsoft PowerPoint helps you easily capture, synchronize, and publish audio, video, slides, and images. Microsoft Producer is also widely used in organizations that have the need to create presentations with large collaboration needs and complex requirements in a short time frame. It also complies with e-learning standards developed by Instructional Management Systems (IMS) Global Learning Consortium, Inc., and the U.S. Department of Defense Sharable Content Object Reference Model (SCORM).

As with all Microsoft products, Producer closely integrates with other Microsoft technologies such as Windows Media, which makes video capture and encoding simple and fast. It also allows you to import rich-media presentations created with Producer directly into your Microsoft FrontPage Web site. Once a presentation has been created, you also have the ability to publish presentations to a Microsoft Windows SharePoint Services site with just a few clicks. This creates greater distribution reach and the ability to search for presentations by title, author, and description.

The wizard templates in Producer allow detailed customization of your presentation, yet keep it simple and easy to manage. Such detailed options include the ability to switch between multiple layouts during the course of a presentation to engage the viewer and the ability to narrate slides without needing to first drop the PowerPoint presentation on the time line.

Creating rich-media presentations with video and reducing your post-production time has never been easier thanks to today's technological tools. It is now possible to quickly create customized presentations by accessing numerous options with simple-to-use wizards. If you're contemplating adding video to your next presentation, there is no better time than now to test some of the available options in the marketplace. With a little practice, these products will allow even the most untechnical executive to take his presentation to the next level with video interactivity.

You don't have to be a media and entertainment company or an independent filmmaker to acquire the power of creating more compelling content in a shorter amount of time. No matter the type of content, the size of a company, or the means of Internet delivery, streaming and digital media solutions are making the process more efficient and easier to leverage.

7.3 Using media as part of a customized Web portal to increase sales and improve customer satisfaction

Streaming media directly impacts increasing sales and improves customer service differently than once thought. Most people associate increasing sales on the Web with increasing the volume of sales. While that always helps, many companies use streaming and digital media to increase revenue by creating more profit on their products by reducing overhead costs and improving customer satisfaction. In many cases, if you can reduce the cost of supporting the products you already sold and continue to sell, the overall margins on the sales will continue to climb. This earns more profit whether the volume of sales increases or not.

One company—Mercedes-Benz USA (MBUSA), the automotive marketing subsidiary of DaimlerChrysler Holding Company—provides marketing services, sales programs, and technician training to 313 Mercedes-Benz dealerships. Mercedes-Benz automobiles are among the top-selling luxury brands in the United States, and their market position continues to grow. Along with sales growth, their automobile technology systems continue to advance and are now considered among the most sophisticated in the world. The rapid growth and complex systems put strains upon recruiting efforts and training capacity, but MBUSA is committed to maintaining a high degree of customer satisfaction to ensure that capacity pressures never affect high standards in dealership personnel and technician training programs.

In response to growth pressures, MBUSA's Technical Training department focused on effective and efficient ways to meet customer needs. Taking advantage of the Web and an existing Windows-based dealership extranet, the Technical Training group developed information access and e-learning programs using Microsoft Windows Media. Streamed information access and e-learning programs provide enhanced customer satisfaction and substantial cost savings in terms of travel, salaries, and lost technician productivity, which equals a higher profit on each car sold.

MBUSA's Technical Training department is located in Montvale, New Jersey, with four regional education centers dispersed throughout the United States. The department is responsible for training dealership technicians on new model diagnostic and disassembly procedures, maintenance, and general and collision repair for Mercedes-Benz passenger cars and M-class light trucks, and technician certification for the STARMARK pre-owned program. Each technician must have familiarity with, and ready access to, information about current model years as well as maintenance and repair details for past models. Prior to this solution, MBUSA delivered all training at their education centers or through videotaped and printed self-study materials. Each procedure video or course preparation document was created or updated and then duplicated and shipped to the retail centers.

Although MBUSA anticipated ongoing costs when updating technical information, it sought a method that would reduce actual expenditures and eliminate a hidden cost—ensuring that all obsolete information was properly discarded and that technicians had uninterrupted access to the new material. MBUSA also needed to alleviate classroom capacity pressures and deliver timely educational content directly to the technician. The new method had to minimize technician travel away from dealerships, provide greater access to new training and certification material, lower the total cost of distribution, and provide students with pre-classroom preparation and post-classroom training support.

In addition to the need for efficient training methods, Mercedes-Benz dealers continually seek the best and brightest talent to fulfill customer expectations and service demands. In an effort to enhance recruitment efforts, MBUSA pursued creative methods to introduce potential dealership employees to the company's history, its products, and the opportunities available at Mercedes-Benz dealerships. MBUSA developed communication, information access, and e-learning programs enhanced by the power of streaming media. Servers running Microsoft Windows 2000 and Windows Media services were installed to stream on-demand content to 313 dealer sites and to technicians' homes via dial-up or broadband systems.

Now from their homes or dealership desktops, using Web-based content enhanced with streaming media, technicians prepare for classroom instruction, access up-to-date model component information such as disassembly and the theory behind vehicle systems operation, and reinforce instruction following classroom sessions. The Technical Training department continues to move appropriate certification and training courses out of the classroom and onto the network. Currently, technicians can become certified to perform STARMARK pre-owned vehicle inspections by using a Windows Media enhanced, interactive application on the company's extranet. Other efficiency breakthroughs include migration of component disassembly information for all current production vehicles to a library of current, indexed Windows Media files. In many cases, Windows Media-based e-learning provides an "on-demand" instructor who can demonstrate repair procedures and techniques realistically, when and where a technician needs to see them.

Mercedesbenzcareers.com attracts new dealership recruits with the help of streaming video presentations from actual dealership employees. The online information is refreshed regularly and used extensively as a part of recruitment activities that occur at auto shows, vocational schools, and events for transitioning military personnel. E-learning programs and recruitment efforts enhanced with streaming media are expected to benefit MBUSA and Mercedes-Benz dealerships considerably in terms of travel, instructor time, technician wages and productivity, facility overhead, and, most importantly, customer satisfaction.

Clearly, streaming media-based systems have the ability to help companies develop, implement, and deploy internal and external systems to improve the bottom line, and more important, enhance customer service.

7.4 Putting your knowledge into action

Now that you have a basic understanding of what it takes to successfully implement a streaming and digital media-based system, it's time to put that knowledge into action. Today there are strong touchpoints as to the direct return on investment (ROI) you can achieve from digital media systems, and no matter the vertical or size of your organization, you can and will see positive results. Even after reading this book, the process can feel overwhelming, especially if this is your first time working with digital media. Remember that there are plenty of free resources available to assist you (see the beginning of the book, page 8) and many providers who are willing to help educate you on the process. It is not as difficult, time-consuming, or expensive as you may think and as some make it out to be. (If you have additional questions or comments on the book or need answers to some direct questions, there is contact information listed in the Introduction.)

Good luck streaming!

7.5 Case studies

7.5.1 MasterCard

MasterCard International is a global payments company with one of the most recognized brands in the world. Founded in 1966, the company has approximately 25,000 members and more than 29 million acceptance locations. It serves consumers and businesses in 210 countries and territories. Today, the company's brands—MasterCard, Cirrus, and Maestro—are found on more than 1.7 billion credit, charge, and debit cards in circulation.

MasterCard International is also a recognized leader in technology and innovation. The company operates Banknet, one of the world's largest global telecommunications networks. Its virtual private network, which updates Banknet to link new areas of the world to the global payments infrastructure, is the first such network in the industry.

The need

MasterCard International uses meetings to disseminate information and promote real-time interaction between employees and executives. However, with approximately 4,000 employees in more than 47 offices around the world, gathering people in one location can be prohibitively expensive and time-consuming. Even meetings confined to employees in a single city can mean taking everyone off site for several hours and arranging for an auditorium, transportation, equipment, and food. E-mail, although a useful tool in some instances, lacks the intensity and interactivity of face-to-face encounters. MasterCard International needed a more efficient and cost-effective way to communicate with its employees, whether in a single location or worldwide, without losing the emotional, personal, and interactive nature of face-to-face meetings. The company also wanted to accommodate those who might be traveling or telecommuting, as well as those who work second or third shifts.

The solution

After evaluating a range of products, MasterCard International chose to work with RealNetworks (www.realnetworks.com) streaming media technology for much of the company's internal communications. RealNetworks technology was compatible with the company's existing systems and infrastructure. The company also needed a system that could span a variety of viewer connection speeds. RealAudio and RealVideo were chosen because their compression capabilities allowed large files to be compressed and moved around quickly and easily. Streaming media technology delivered to MasterCard the ability to produce more effective internal communications by providing the means to engage employees in personal, interactive meetings without the expense, complexity, and productivity loss associated with having all participants present in one location at one time.

Recently, MasterCard International completed the largest structural event in its history, the integration of its European organization into the parent company. To celebrate, the company held a global webcast in which participants in St. Louis, Missouri; Purchase, New York; and Brussels, Belgium, were networked together via live streaming video and audio. To set up what MasterCard International billed as their "Integration Celebration," the staff at RealNetworks Consulting Services helped plan the event, determined the right components, deployed and tested the equipment, and figured out how far they could push the system (which was much further than MasterCard International had anticipated). Thousands of employees joined the celebration at the event locations, via their desktops, or by telecommuting. They could see and hear their colleagues, send e-mails, ask questions, and even participate in a worldwide toast. According to MasterCard International, the production was flawless.

For individuals viewing an archived or live event at speeds of 56 Kbps and beyond, for those working off site, for centrally located groups, and for those at worldwide all-hands meetings, RealNetworks streaming media technology delivered steady, uninterrupted video and audio to every participant.

For MasterCard International streaming media technology can also:

- Help the user see and hear the presenter and experience the emotions, expressions, enthusiasm, and sensitivity of the department head or executive in a way not possible with e-mails or conference calls
- Offer immediate feedback by answering pop-up questionnaires and post-meeting surveys
- Ask questions and receive answers in real time by e-mailing questions to an event moderator who relays them to the presenter
- View associated materials at the same time, including PowerPoint slides, language translations, etc.
- Review archived versions of a meeting or presentation from anywhere at any time

The deployment

A different technology was used to deploy MasterCard's "Integration Celebration."

- RealNetworks server intranet: Redundant servers at each major location for fail-safe live broadcasting via a wide range of connection speeds
- RealNetworks Producer Plus: Redundant copies at each major location for fail-safe encoding of both live and on-demand viewing
- RealOne Player: Deployed on all MasterCard International workstations, allowing employees to view content from their desktops
- Hardware: IBM 324, 325, and 360 servers
- Operating system: Microsoft Windows 2000
- Connectivity: 7-Mb ATM and 3-Mb Frame Circuit connections between major offices in St. Louis, Missouri; Purchase, New York; and Brussels, Belgium. T1 lines to smaller regional offices

Mission accomplished

By deploying streaming media technology, MasterCard International now reaches more people for less money. Today, the company can reach more employees at any given time anywhere in the world. In the past, a traditional company meeting could only accommodate about 400 or 500 employees at a time. Now nearly 4,000 employees can see and hear the same messages. Employees feel more involved and connected to the streaming messages delivered. Participants can interact in real time and meetings are less disruptive because participants can access live and archived events while on the road, at home, at their desktop, or just about anywhere with an Internet connection.

In the past, numerous meetings called for renting halls and equipment, arranging transportation, providing food and accommodations, coordinating busy schedules, and generally disrupting the lives of all involved. These were expensive affairs. By taking advantage of RealNetworks technology, MasterCard had a better ROI and reduced meeting costs by more than 65 percent.

After a recent "face-to-face" meeting utilizing RealNetworks technology, participants were asked about the use of streaming media. In response, 100 percent of the participants agreed that streaming video was a good medium for company-wide meetings. In addition, 100 percent of the respondents rated the video and audio quality as "excellent." (For more information on this case study please, visit www.realnetworks.com.)

7.5.2 Wisconsin Department of Transportation streams historic bridge float

December 17, 2003, was a typical winter day in La Crosse, Wisconsin. The thermometer hovered in the single digits most of the day. The ground was covered in a few inches of fresh snow and large chunks of ice floated in the Mississippi River. This typical day became remarkable when the Wisconsin Department of Transportation (WisDOT) attempted a rare civil engineering feat and let the whole world watch.

This feat involved floating the fully constructed arch for the new Coulee Crossing Bridge across the Mississippi River and then connecting it to permanent bridge piers. The mammoth arch is 475 feet long, 50 feet wide, and 87 feet high. It is comprised of 2.8 million pounds of steel held together with more than 28,000 field bolts. Once completed, the entire bridge will span 2,573 feet. The event marked just the second time in civil engineering history that a bridge structure of this size was pre-constructed along the shoreline and then floated into place.

Using Sonic Foundry's (www.sonicfoundry.com) Mediasite, WisDOT was able to chronicle the historical event in full audio and video with graphics and stream it live and on-demand to online viewers watching from home or work. At just under 10 hours, it was the longest single live event ever webcast using Mediasite. From that footage, the department also created a condensed version.

"We wanted to create a documentary of sorts to show not only what was happening that day, but to capture the historical importance of it all," said

Don Hartman, engineering communications specialist with WisDOT. "From an engineering perspective, we wanted to show what we were doing, why we were doing it, and how we were doing it, and then share that with other districts here in Wisconsin as well as with DOTs in other states. We also wanted to capture what the bridge means to the La Crosse community."

In addition to time-sequenced shots of the bridge float, the rich-media webcast featured artist renderings, engineering diagrams, and photographs detailing the progression of the construction project, as well as interviews with department staff, civil engineers, and construction crew members. Local elected officials, government agency representatives, and La Crosse area residents also shared their perspectives. Some of the interviews were conducted live and at the scene; others were taped a few weeks in advance.

Whereas most webcasts are simple video presentations with a speaker and PowerPoint slides, WisDOT took advantage of Mediasite's unique dual-channel, real-time processor that captures and encodes all RGB-source graphics to push the limits of rich-media Web communications. Using a five-cameraman crew, WisDOT began shooting at 6:00 a.m. on the day of the float. Mediasite captured, synchronized, and streamed the audio and video from the five cameramen plus the taped interviews and supporting collateral and images.

"This was the first time we'd ever done a webcast, and it was a pretty complicated one at that, but Mediasite worked perfectly," said Hartman. "Even after using it just one time, my creative juices started flowing as I thought about all the different uses we could find for it. The Department of Administration has a Mediasite unit and now we can't wait to get one. I think the whole event, being so different from anything they've done before, even opened Sonic Foundry's eyes to the potential of its product."

Without streaming media, there would be no cost-effective way to share this monumental event with the general public, transportation partners, and government leaders. In reality, WisDOT not only saved travel costs by enabling employees in other districts to watch online versus traveling to La Crosse, but it was able to share the event with a much larger audience.

"We always planned to produce a video documenting the arch move, but it would have taken us two months to edit it, which kind of takes away from some of the excitement of the day," said Hartman. "People want to see it NOW and through the magic of streaming media, we were able to share this historic event LIVE with the whole world. It was an amazing day."

The whole world may not have tuned in, but the live and on-demand audiences were still much larger than expected. Sonic Foundry hosted the webcast and it was the company's highest trafficked event to date. The live webcast generated more than 1,500 unique IP views while averaging 356 concurrent connections. Since the event, another 2,100 viewers watched at least part of the webcast on-demand.

"I was getting calls from people all over the state, all over the country really, saying they saw the webcast," said Hartman. "They thought it was really exciting and loved the fact that they could watch it live. I guess it's not every day you see a three million pound bridge moving across the Mississippi River."

Said Gary Snyder, bridge project leader for WisDOT: "The day was a proud moment for WisDOT, and we were amazed by how easily Mediasite allowed us to share it with state and local residents, as well as other state DOTs and anyone else interested in watching. Not only was the webcast a valuable real-time communications tool, but the archive will serve as both an educational and historical rich-media resource for years to come."

With the resounding success of this ambitious pilot project, WisDOT is now looking to use streaming media for additional applications, including internal engineering and project briefings, public hearings on transportation improvement projects, State Highway Patrol Academy training courses, project bid-letting presentations, and internal employee training. By capturing these types of presentations for distribution via the Internet or burned to CDs, WisDOT anticipates significant savings in travel time and expenses while providing broader, more convenient access to department content. The ability to create live and on-demand Web presentations also will extend the department's reach and enable increased feedback from transportation customers via Mediasite's interactive polling and Q&A capabilities. (For more information on this case study please visit www.sonicfoundry.com.)

APPENDIX A

Uses of Streaming and Digital Media Report

In July 2003, the Aberdeen Group and Streaming Media, Inc., administered two separate surveys to streamingmedia.com Web site visitors. The surveys asked respondents how they used streaming and digital media in both a business and personal context. It also asked them about how they used rich media including frequency, session length, and preferred media players. This report summarized the survey responses and provided Aberdeen's analysis of the data. Most important, this report translated that data analysis into specific recommendations and streaming digital media has directly impacted enterprises, content providers, and end users.

We have included the Executive Summary of that report, which gives the facts and figures based on the survey findings. More information about the entire 70-page report is available at www.streamingmedia.com/research.

Statistically significant research data

Unlike many surveys conducted in the past on streaming and digital media, the Aberdeen Group surveys have a statistically significant respondent base. Thus, the results and analysis are defensible as an empirical benchmark against which readers can gauge their own use of business and personal applications and upon which future trend analysis can be conducted.

The streamingmedia.com Web site receives more than 45,000 unique visits per month, with more than 25,500 individuals receiving its weekly newsletter, *Streaming Media Xtra*. The survey, created by the Aberdeen Group, received 918 valid responses; the survey created by streamingmedia. com received 2,043 valid responses. Those levels provide a 99 percent confidence level with a confidence interval of +3 percent. In other words, the responses to the survey represent the population of streamingmedia.com.

The next logical question is: Does the streamingmedia.com population represent the general public, buyers of the streaming technologies, Web surfers, or some other subgroup of the general population? The respondent overview in Chapter 2 of the report presents the aggregated demographics of the respondent base. Individual readers of the entire report should use Chapter 2 to determine how close the respondent base is to their target population: internal users, external customers, or potential buyers of technologies and services.

The Aberdeen Group performed all of the analysis and recommendations included in their report. They analyzed the data as a total group and in several subgroups—company size and interest group—which is how the respondents themselves classified their "interest in streaming and digital media" per a specific survey question. The subgroup analysis is not as statistically significant as the overall data set; the confidence level for some of these subgroups drops to 95 percent. Chapter 2 presents the response levels of the subgroups. Readers should use Chapter 2 of the report to determine the statistical significance of any specific subgroups in comparison with the aggregated data.

Findings contained in the report

The Aberdeen report contains statistically significant measurements of:

- Usage rates of business and personal applications that involve streaming and digital media, with segment analysis by company size and interest group for now and for the next 12 months
- Planned spending on streaming and outsourced technologies, services, and applications for the next 12 months
- For business respondents, the percentage of company sites currently enabled for streaming or digital media
- User frequency and session length of streaming media sessions, with segment analysis by company size and interest group
- Media player installed base and user preference
- Adoption rates of file sharing, subscription, and for-pay content services

Each of the data sets is presented in table or graph format and includes Aberdeen's analysis of what is important or noteworthy. Aberdeen also highlights the relevant implications, recommendations, and impact for enterprises, content providers, and end users.

Aberdeen believes their report is the first statistically valid benchmark of the streaming and rich-media market. Although the population for this study may not represent 100 percent of the market at large, it is highly representative of individuals, businesses, and suppliers that have an active interest in streaming and digital media.

Executive summary

Streaming and digital media are ready for prime time

Aberdeen has followed the technologies and services that make up the streaming and digital media marketplace for the last four years. In Aberdeen's analysis, the market has gone from hype (1999) to hurt (2001) to helpful (2003). Over this period, some companies jumped in feet first, only to find that technologies and users were not mature enough to effectively use the media. In this report, Aberdeen proves that now is the time to aggressively engage, or re-engage, in streaming and digital media for business and personal applications, cost savings, revenue opportunities, and customer interaction. This claim has been made before; however, Aberdeen's numbers are new. This statistically valid benchmark study points the way to streaming and digital media success and reveals the following findings:

- A mature, experienced user base now exists. Enterprises and content providers can now confidently deploy streaming and digital media knowing that internal employees and external customers have solid experience with media in a variety of contexts.
- Firms that have deployed streaming applications in some business areas (e.g., distance learning, webcasting) should look to other applications (e.g., product launches, executive communications) that build on those successes.
- Company executives, IT professionals, and content providers who are dabbling in media usage should move full-force toward expanding their deployments.

This report has real numbers to show that users are actively using the available streaming and digital media applications. The Executive Summary highlights the key findings from this report in relation to business applications and use, personal applications and use, and overall media usage.

Highlights of business application usage

The following section summarizes the top-level findings for business application usage from the survey results.

Business applications with media approaching 50 percent adoption in the coming year

Most business applications with streaming or digital media components have a solid current use: 25–35 percent of respondents regularly use rich media in company meetings, distance learning, external corporate announcements, and internal executive communications. Respondents also show a consistent projected adoption of business applications with streaming or digital media over the next 12 months, with total potential usage approaching 50 percent of users.

Contrary to expectations, sales force training trails most other business applications, with a little more than 20 percent of respondents reporting current use and only 38 percent indicating potential adoption of these applications in the next 12 months. Vendors regularly tout sales force training as the largest category, which is not the case. In reality, webcasting and Web conferencing are the leading business applications for streaming and digital media.

Enterprises should compare their current use of these applications with the survey results and ask themselves: Am I a leader or a laggard? Leaders in one application should examine other applications with similar adoption rates for opportunities to increase the leverage of their IT investments in digital media. Laggards can use this analysis to determine where to start.

Spending on media applications in 2004 is not strong

Despite the economic upturn, suppliers in the streaming and digital media industry should plan on another tough year. Survey respondents said that their average spending per company for the coming year will be less than $100,000 for products and services and less than $50,000 for outsourced broadcast services. Only 5 percent of respondents expect to spend more than $1 million in the next 12 months.

Aberdeen research indicated that at least part of this low projected spending level is caused by the milestone approach to IT spending: Buyers may plan for the overall investment, but they do not commit real dollars until specified milestones are reached. They purchase for one location or one application, get results from that segment, and then spend more only if the results are positive. Spending per company for the coming year will be less than $100,000 for products and services and less than $50,000 for outsourced broadcast services.

Highlights of personal application usage

The following summarizes the top-level findings for personal application usage from the survey results.

Media and entertainment dominate personal uses

The online versions of entertainment, news, and media content—news sites, movie trailers, and streaming radio—have the highest uptake, with more than 50 percent of respondents using these applications. Traditional "for-pay" categories such as games and sports have the lowest uptake, with less than 10 percent of respondent usage. Although only 27 percent of respondents indicated that they belong to subscription services, more than 60 percent have paid for online content.

These findings indicate that the best personal use of media applications is to augment other forms of media and entertainment. Subscriptions are a viable method to gather an audience, but should not be relied upon as the primary method for distributing content.

Highlights of overall media usage

The following summarizes the top-level findings for overall media usage from the survey results.

Media use is a regular occurrence among all users

Enterprises can expect their users are already familiar with accessing media on their desktops. The survey shows that more than 50 percent of respondents use streaming or digital content at least once a day. Nearly 75 percent of respondents use online media at least two to three times per week, which includes the business user subsegment. As a result, enterprises can be confident that the majority of their users (both employees and end customers) are comfortable using media on their computers for both business and personal applications. This finding opens the door for expanding the use of network-delivered media in an enterprise without fear that transitioning from traditional broadcast, videotape, or other forms of delivery will decrease usability.

Users are conditioned to use media for short spurts

Despite the familiarity, most users are not ready to spend long periods of time consuming media on the desktop. The survey shows that users access media in short spurts, with nearly 65 percent of the respondents spending 30 minutes or less per session.

The implication for businesses is not that longer content won't be watched: The survey did not ask about preferences for this topic, only about current habits. However, to conform to current usage patterns, enterprises should cut longer media into segments that are consumable in stages.

All players are installed, but Microsoft is preferred

Enterprises and content providers can rest assured that users will be able to access media in almost any format. Microsoft Windows Media is the leading installer of media players, with a 95 percent installed base. RealPlayer is close behind with an 87 percent installed base, and QuickTime has 83 percent. When it comes to which player users prefer, though, Microsoft is the clear leader. Users reported a two to one preference for Windows Media over RealPlayer or QuickTime.

Companies should continue making player and media server choices based on which technology best fits the needs of the application and provides the highest return on investment. Although users are comfortable with all players, to please the greatest number of users, companies should choose Microsoft technologies—as long as the business case does not preclude Windows Media because of cost, customizability, or other requirements.

Media usage and preferences

This section presents the research findings, analysis, and impact of survey responses in the following subject areas:

- Frequency of media use
- Length of media sessions
- Media players installed
- Preferred media player

Frequency of media use

These data are presented in three ways: all respondents, segmented by company size, and segmented by interest group (as classified by the respondents). The Aberdeen survey asked respondents the following question: How often do you use streaming media or digital media (audio or video streamed or downloaded over a network or the Internet) either for personal or business use?

a. Once per month
b. Two to three times per month
c. Once per week
d. Two to three times per week
e. Once per day
f. More than once per day

Figure A.1 summarizes the aggregated responses to this question, Figure A.2 segments responses by company size, and Figure A.3 segments respondents by interest group.

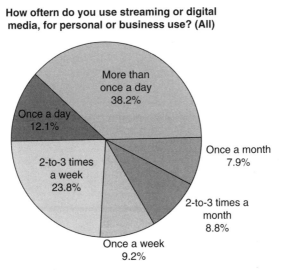

Source: Aberdeen Group, January 2004

Figure A.1: *Frequency of use, all respondents—Most users access media at least two to three times per week.*

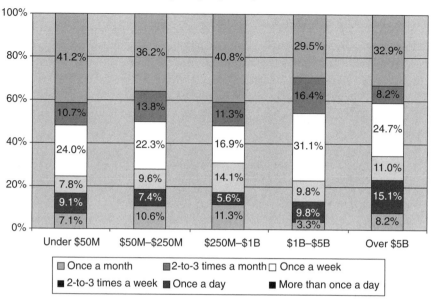

How often do you use streaming or digital media?
(Company Size)

Source: Aberdeen Group, January 2004

Figure A.2: *Frequency of use, company size—Respondents at smaller companies are likely to use media more frequently than at larger companies.*

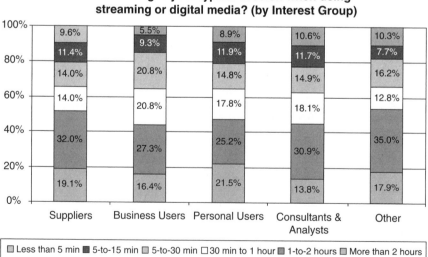

How long is your typical session when using
streaming or digital media? (by Interest Group)

Source: Aberdeen Group, January 2004

Figure A.3: *Frequency of use, interest group—Most groups use streaming and digital media several times per week. Outside of the supplier community, daily use is less common.*

All respondents

Research finding: More than 50 percent of respondents access streaming or digital media content at least once a day. Nearly 75 percent of respondents use online media at least 2–3 times a week (see Figure A.1).

    Analysis: There is an audience that is experienced and comfortable with accessing and consuming digital media content over the Internet and IP networks.

    Impact: This is great news for content providers and for businesses. When this research is combined with the recent Arbitron Inc./Edison Media Research finding that residential broadband penetration has reached 21 percent of the United States population, it indicates that an end-user market of significant size and frequency of use now exists to create a profitable business for a mass consumer market. This is good news for everyone but content providers. For businesses, the frequency indicates that users are achieving a solid experience and comfort level with streaming and digital media. That should help prevent the underlying technologies from inhibiting usage of corporate streaming media applications. That is a big leap from the previous situation, where the new technologies caused more problems than they solved.

Company size

Research finding: More than half of the respondents in the small company segments said that they use media at least once per day. Respondents in less than half of the large company segments use media at least once per day. Seventy-five percent of all segments approached or exceed usage of more than two to three times per week (Figure A.2).

    Analysis: Users at companies of all sizes commonly use streaming and digital media. There is a higher frequency in smaller companies.

    Impact: Enterprises who consider expanding their streaming and digital media programs can be assured that, because of regular usage, their users are already quite comfortable with the format.

Interest group

Research finding: Suppliers are by far the largest users of streaming and digital media, with 64 percent of supplier respondents using media at least once per day. Few personal users access media on a daily basis (more than 33 percent), but 65 percent access media two to three times per week (Figure A.3).

    Analysis: Although company size closely reflects the aggregate data, there are significant variations when examining the data by interest group. Personal users, who are expected to be the largest user group, don't access media as often as suppliers. Business users, presumed to be enterprise or corporate users who are not suppliers of streaming and digital media technologies and services, have a strong base.

Impact: It is no surprise that suppliers use streaming and digital media the most often. It is surprising, however, that the business group uses media more frequently than personal users. One implication is that businesses are requiring more use of streaming and digital media, which drives up the frequency of use. However, no correlation analysis has been performed at this time to associate business applications to business usage, although this analysis is available upon request.

Session length of streaming and digital media

The Aberdeen survey asked respondents the following question: How long is your typical session when using streaming or digital media?

a. Less than 5 minutes
b. 5 to 15 minutes
c. 15 to 30 minutes
d. 30 minutes to 1 hour
e. 1 to 2 hours
f. More than 2 hours

Figure A.4 summarizes the aggregated responses to this question, Figure A.5 segments responses by company size, and Figure A.6 segments respondents by interest group.

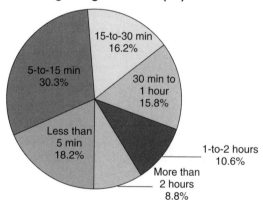

How long is your typical session when using streaming or digital media? (All)

15-to-30 min 16.2%

30 min to 1 hour 15.8%

5-to-15 min 30.3%

Less than 5 min 18.2%

1-to-2 hours 10.6%

More than 2 hours 8.8%

Source: Aberdeen Group, January 2004

Figure A.4: *Length of session, all respondents—More users access shorter media segments.*

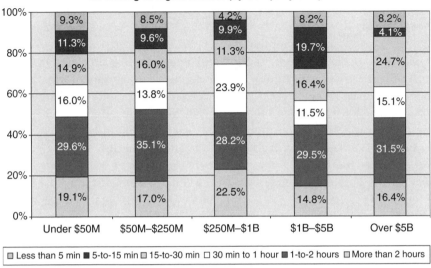

Figure A.5: *Session length, company size and interest group—Segmentation analysis of session length does not vary significantly from the aggregate data set.*

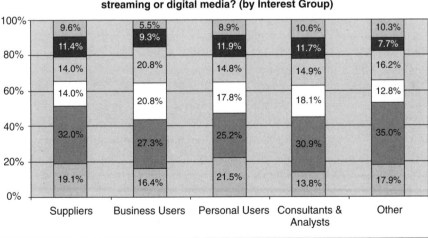

Figure A.6

All respondents

Research finding: Forty-eight percent of respondents indicated that they use streaming or digital media for 15 minutes or less per session. Nearly 65 percent of respondents said that they spend 30 minutes or less per session. Only 19.4 percent will spend more than 1 hour per session (Figure A.4).

Analysis: Users are currently conditioned to consume short-format audio and video over IP networks. It is not clear from the research whether this results from a chicken-and-the-egg problem: Do respondents use short format because they prefer it or because that is all that is available?

Impact: The impact here is somewhat uncertain. The current prevalence of short-format use indicates that the longer the audio or video content, the smaller the base of consumers who are willing to watch/listen to the entire program. Therefore, to reach the largest audience, business- and consumer-oriented companies should create content that is less than 15 minutes. Longer content may be able to reach the large audience if it is broken into discrete, sub-15-minute segments that can easily be stopped, restarted, and skipped. However, given that the analysis neither asked respondents how long they are willing to use digital media nor correlated availability with usage, the issue needs further research before any strong conclusions can be drawn.

Company size and interest group

Research finding: In terms of session length, both company size analysis and interest group analysis echo the aggregate data set (Figures A.5 and A.6).

Analysis: The lack of significant variation by company size or interest group contains the same ambiguity as the aggregate: Is there no variation because only short-form content is available or because users prefer shorter content? This is a question for future analysis.

Impact: It would be premature to advise particular actions based on these data. However, content providers, enterprises, and suppliers can infer that most users are conditioned to consume content that is less than 30 minutes in length. This conditioning should be taken into account when designing new streaming or digital media services. Anything longer than 30 minutes may necessitate behavioral changes for the general user, which can increase the challenge to market acceptance and wide user adoption.

Media players installed

The Aberdeen and streamingmedia.com surveys both asked respondents the following question: Which of the following media players do you have installed on your desktop?

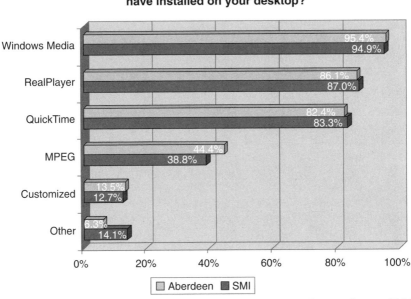

Which of the following media players do you have installed on your desktop?

Source: Aberdeen Group and streamingmedia.com, January 2004

Figure A.7: *Media players all respondents, installed.*

a. Windows Media Player from Microsoft
b. RealPlayer from RealNetworks
c. QuickTime Player from Apple
d. MPEG player
e. Customized player
f. Other

Figure A.7 summarizes the responses to the surveys.

All respondents

Findings: Microsoft has the highest installed penetration among respondents; nearly 95 percent reported that Windows Media Player is installed on their desktops. RealPlayer is close behind with an 87 percent installed base, and QuickTime has 83%. MPEG players are installed on nearly 39 percent of desktops, and customized players are installed on less than 13 percent of desktops (Figure A.5).

Analysis: Most users have several media players installed. Without multiple surveys conducted over several intervals, it is not possible to determine if any of the players' installed bases are growing or shrinking. This analysis will be conducted in future studies.

Impact: Aberdeen research shows that, behind the firewall, most companies choose one format and require their users to view content in that format. The high installed base of all three players, Microsoft, RealPlayer, and QuickTime, guarantees that choosing any one of these formats will address a broad base of users who already have the player available. Companies that want to please the largest number of current users and deliver content in the widest preferred format should offer their content in the Microsoft format. This research does not correlate cost of delivery with format of delivery. Companies evaluating streaming media platforms should also evaluate the licensing and maintenance costs of all available options before selecting a specific media format.

Company size

Findings and analysis (Figure A.8, with the SMI survey responses):

* Microsoft's Windows Media Player remains the leader in all segments, with a low of 95.2 percent in the less than $50 million segment and a high of 97.9 percent in the $1 to $5 billion segment.
* RealNetworks' RealPlayer rises slightly over the aggregated data set in two segments, reaching a 90.3 percent installed base in the $250 million to $1 billion segment and a 91.5 percent installed base in the $1 to $5 billion segment. RealNetworks falls slightly in two segments, dropping to

Media Players Installed, by Company Size

	Under $50 M	$50 M–$250 M	$250 M–$1 B	$1 B–$5 B	Over $5 B
Windows Media Player	95.2%	96.5%	96.0%	97.9%	97.1%
RealPlayer	86.8%	83.2%	90.3%	91.5%	83.5%
QuickTime Player	84.5%	77.7%	82.3%	84.0%	74.1%
MPEG Player	45.4%	40.1%	41.9%	51.1%	38.8%
Customized Player	13.9%	10.4%	12.1%	16.0%	12.2%
Other	6.9%	3.0%	4.0%	8.5%	5.0%

Source: streamingmedia.com, January 2004.

Figure A.8: *Media players installed, company size—Mostly mirror aggregate data set, with variances.*

an 83.2 percent installed base in the $50 to $250 million segment and an 83.5 percent installed base in the more than $5 billion segment.

- Apple QuickTime reflects the aggregate for three segments (less than $50 million: 84.5 percent; $250 million to $1 billion: 82.3 percent; and $1 to 5 billion: 84 percent). Apple falls in the other segments to 77.7 percent in the $50 to 250 million segment and to 74.1 percent in the more than $5 billion segment.
- The MPEG player reflects the aggregate data set, except for a significant jump in the $1 to 5 billion segment, which reaches 51.1 percent.
- The customized player and other categories see no significant difference from the aggregate data set.

Impact: Enterprises should work with application developers to determine the most appropriate platform for their internal content and applications.

Interest group

Findings and analysis (see Figure A.9, with the SMI responses):

- Microsoft's Windows Media Player remains the leader in all interest group segments and does not vary significantly from the aggregate results (from 94.9 to 96.6 percent).
- RealNetworks' RealOne Player remains steady for the supplier and business user segments (87.7 and 86.1 percent, respectively), but drops to 83.5 percent in the consultant/analyst segment and to 81.6 percent in the personal user segment.

Media Players Installed, by Company Group

	Suppliers	Business	Personal	Consultants	Other
Windows Media Player	96.6%	94.9%	96.0%	96.3%	91.8%
RealPlayer	87.7%	86.1%	81.6%	83.5%	86.0%
QuickTime Player	84.4%	82.1%	81.6%	79.4%	79.8%
MPEG Player	46.7%	44.6%	37.6%	44.5%	39.5%
Customized Player	16.2%	11.2%	7.2%	12.8%	14.4%
Other	7.7%	5.3%	8.0%	4.1%	5.3%

Source: streamingmedia.com, January 2004.

Figure A.9: *Media players installed, interest group—Mostly mirror aggregate data set, with variances.*

- Apple QuickTime is steady, with a high of 84.4 percent in the supplier segment and a low of 79.4 percent in the consultant/analyst segment.
- The MPEG player is also steady, with a low of 37.6 percent of the personal users and a high of 47.6 percent among suppliers.
- The customized player and other categories see no significant difference from the aggregate data set.

Additional analysis and impact studies of the installed base of media players are available upon request from Aberdeen.

Impact: The drop against the aggregated data set in the installed base of RealPlayer and QuickTime in the personal segment indicates that, if enterprises or content providers want to reach the widest possible audience, they should use the Microsoft platform. Again, further research is required to determine the growth pattern of any of these installed base segments.

Media players: preferred

The Aberdeen survey asked respondents the following question: If given a choice, which format do you prefer to use?

a. MPEG player
b. QuickTime (Apple)
c. RealMedia (RealNetworks)
d. Windows Media (Microsoft)
e. Other

Figure A.10 summarizes the aggregated responses to the survey.

All respondents

Findings: Microsoft was selected as the preferred player by 40 percent of all respondents. RealPlayer edged out QuickTime for second place, as these players finished with 22 and 21 percent, respectively. MPEG players garnered only 12 percent of player preference (Figure A.10).

Analysis: Microsoft is clearly the player of choice and has the highest penetration rate. The near-even split between RealPlayer and QuickTime is interesting but only a starting point for further research. Tracking this question over time will provide better insight into whether Apple will overtake RealNetworks, or if format preferences have reached stabilization.

Impact: When combined with the installed base results, this question reinforces the recommendation that enterprises and content providers that seek to reach the widest possible audience should use Windows Media format. RealPlayer and QuickTime are also important options, particularly for content providers trying to please the majority of the potential users base.

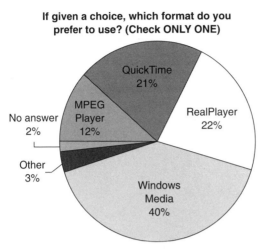

If given a choice, which format do you prefer to use? (Check ONLY ONE)

Source: Aberdeen Group, January 2004

Figure A.10: *Media player preferred, all respondents—Microsoft has a significant lead. QuickTime and RealPlayer are practically equal.*

Company size

Findings and analysis (Figure A.11, from Aberdeen survey):

- Microsoft's Windows Media Player remains the preferred player in all segments. There is a significant jump over the aggregate data set in the $1 to $5 billion subsegment, with a preference of 49.2 percent. There is a less significant but still relevant bump in the $50 to $250 million segment to 45.2 percent.
- Preference for RealPlayer reflects the aggregate data, with the exception of the $250 million to $1 billion segment, where preference rises to 27.5 percent.
- Preference for QuickTime remains steady in most company segments, but drops to 14.8 percent in the largest segment.
- There is no significant difference based on company size in preference for MPEG player over the aggregated data set.

Impact: The sharp increase in preference for Microsoft in the top segment is significant, which indicates that Microsoft has a controlling critical mass in this segment. Further study is required to determine the source of the jump and whether the difference will hold with a broader data set than the streamingmedia.com respondents.

Media Players Preferred, by Company Size

	Under $50 M	$50 M–$250 M	$250 M–$1 B	$1 B–$5 B	Over $5 B
MPEG Player	12.2%	10.8%	10.1%	9.8%	13.7%
QuickTime Player	23.9%	20.4%	18.8%	14.8%	17.8%
RealPlayer	21.2%	21.5%	27.5%	23.0%	19.2%
Windows Media	39.3%	45.2%	40.6%	49.2%	43.8%
Other	3.3%	2.2%	2.9%	3.3%	5.5%

Source: Aberdeen Group, January 2004.

Figure A.11: *Media players preferred, company size—Mostly mirror aggregate data set, with variances.*

Media Players Preferred, by Interest Group

	Suppliers	Business	Personal	Consultants	Other
MPEG Player	14.0%	11.5%	8.2%	16.3%	4.5%
QuickTime Player	20.5%	17.6%	26.1%	22.8%	23.6%
RealPlayer	20.5%	23.6%	23.9%	18.5%	29.1%
Windows Media	41.8%	43.4%	38.1%	39.1%	39.1%
Other	3.1%	3.8%	3.7%	3.3%	3.6%

Source: Aberdeen Group, January 2004.

Figure A.12: *Media players preferred, interest group—Significant variations from the aggregate.*

Interest group

Data set findings (Figure A.12, from Aberdeen survey):

- Windows Media and RealPlayer preferences by the interest group don't vary significantly from the aggregated data set.
- Preference for QuickTime tracks the aggregate data set, except among personal users, where preference jumps to 26.1 percent. The shift is at the expense of MPEG players, where preference falls to 8.2 percent.

Analysis: The shift in the personal user subsegment from MPEG to Quick-Time is not as significant as the numbers indicate. Because QuickTime is built from the MPEG code base and the informed nature of the respondent base (see Chapter 2), respondents are likely to see both QuickTime and MPEG as two flavors of the same technology. This analysis also reflects other research that indicated that informed user groups see MPEG and QuickTime players as somewhat interchangeable.

Impact: The consistency of results for Microsoft and RealPlayer between the aggregate set and the interest group segments indicates that all users have the same preferences.

APPENDIX B

Enterprise Streaming: Return on Investment Report

Enterprise streaming: return on investment report

We have included a portion of this report, issued by streamingmedia.com, which gives the facts and figures based on how businesses from every industry sector are saving money and generating revenues, using streaming media as a business tool, and how this can help your bottom line. Although some of the data are from 2001 and 2002, they are still relevant to showcase where enterprise streaming is going and how it is getting there. More information on the entire 80-page report is available at www.streamingmedia.com/research.

Report summary

Given the nascent state of enterprise streaming and coordinate lack of tracking information, the primary goal of this research is to identify return on investment (ROI) for corporations employing streaming, and to establish a means of measuring it.

In doing so, we have determined these values of significance: total streaming spending, number of stream-hours delivered, how many people were served, and the duration of streams. We have also formulated new metrics for measuring the costs of streaming in an enterprise. The first thing we noticed when we analyzed our ROI research data was the extremely wide range of uses of streaming within the corporate enterprise. Some companies are spending thousands of dollars annually, and some are investing millions in streaming. Because of this broad spectrum, there is no average example that would be representative or valid. Still, there are specific insights that apply to companies that are just starting to use streaming in training (e-learning) and corporate communications, and to those who have been streaming a long time.

Think of this research report as a family portrait that consists of toddlers through grandparents: Some of the companies we have surveyed have been at it for a long time and some have just started, but most are in between. This report presents an inside view of the varied enterprise uses of streaming, identifies quantifiable and intangible ROI in streaming applications, and provides advice and solutions for those considering a streaming implementation for their company.

Return on investment: identifying and measuring return on investment

Most corporations don't manage ROI for everything they do. For many processes they manage, corporations simply assume that their ROI is acceptable. Do you manage, let's say, the ROI of replacing your employee's PC? It's a simple expense, but because the returns are difficult to track and often qualitative rather than quantitative, they are rarely measured and managed. This is also what happens for streaming.

In the eyes of corporate financial officers, calculating ROI is always about the mix of tangible monetary elements and intangible benefits. The tangible benefits for streaming, in very general terms, are increased revenue and cost savings. Money matters, and it is often the primary goal in the management of corporations. That is why the data analysis in this report is concentrated on spending, revenue, and cost savings.

Many of the benefits of digital media are largely intangible, dealing with matters far harder to measure than the inflow and outflow of money. Still, these intangibles are significant, are often of importance longer term than savings, and are strategic in nature. Managing such intangible benefits requires accurate knowledge about the costs and actual results. Yet, fewer than 5 percent of the companies we interviewed actually try to manage the tangible, let alone intangible, ROI benefits of streaming. This is because streaming ROI benefits are hard to measure. Here are some thoughts on how you can measure your ROI so that you can manage the various benefits of streaming. Remember, you can't manage what you can't measure.

Increased revenue

All companies want to manage the bottom line of net profit. Revenue from specific products and services is relatively easy to measure. But how does your company measure the bottom-line impact of a specific corporate message, an advertising campaign, or a training package? It's extremely difficult to identify the revenue impact of any specific communication. First, give the message an identifier that you can track all the way through to its benefits. For example, in a streamed marketing campaign, include a unique sales code along with the streaming content that the customer provides at the point of sale. Using this technique, you can track a message from your streams all the way through to revenue. Unfortunately, too few companies use simple tracking measures like this.

Cost savings

Few corporations track cost savings. This is potentially very easy to track (rather than sending Sally from New York and Bob from London to Los Angeles, you provide streaming video of the training presentation). But surprisingly, few companies actually measure their cost savings.

Communication

You have important messages and insights for your employees, business partners, and customers. You want to communicate these messages in a way that effectively delivers that meaning and insight. But how can you tell which messages work well and which don't? How can you tell what's been understood and what needs to be clarified? Testing the effectiveness of messages can be relatively easy. Ask the audience a few questions about the central concepts you intended to communicate. Measure the results, and you'll quickly see how well the message was understood. You will also learn which specific audience members could benefit from a better explanation. Again, it's so simple to test the efficacy of messages, yet companies rarely do. Testing every message isn't feasible, but surely some messages are important or complex enough so that measuring how well they are communicated would be worthwhile.

Reach

You want to reach the entire intended audience for your message. Can you really be sure who watched all those videotapes you've been shipping to employees every month? Of course not. Digital media technologies allow you to track exactly who has watched what. Thus, you can measure the reach and manage your assets so that everyone who wasn't reached will be in the future.

Timeliness

You want your messages to reach the audience immediately. In the age of the Internet, traditional media shipping just isn't fast enough. For example, if you just decided to change your business focus or are opening up a new and exciting market, do you really want to wait a month to produce and ship videotapes to everyone you need to reach? Timeliness always matters. Tele-conferencing can get there quickly, but teleconferencing can be costly, won't reach everyone, and can't be indexed for future reference. E-mail is fine, but text will never have the impact or subtlety of audio and video. How can you measure timeliness? Digital media allows you to track how long it took for each intended recipient to view the material.

Productivity

You want to eliminate inefficiencies and unproductive time, and increase the knowledge and skills of your staff. There are many ways to enhance produc-tivity, which include reducing unproductive time while traveling, making smarter decisions more quickly, reducing the number of people required to accomplish a task, accomplishing higher goals that were not previously pos-sible, etc. We spoke with respondents who claimed to have achieved all of these benefits, but few have actually measured them.

Companies must learn to measure and manage their ROI. Because ROI comes in all sizes and flavors, in order to manage it, you must first measure it in all its various forms. Once this is done, a company can truly accomplish its goals.

ROI summary

This research report also identifies several key market segments that rep-resent significant growth opportunity for vendors of enterprise streaming products and services. At the outset, several general indicators about the enterprise streaming market are clear:

- It's just the beginning: Many companies just started streaming in earnest within the past 18 months. Although streaming has been around for almost a decade, it's just now becoming mainstream.
- The big applications: Though the scenarios vary widely, most companies are focusing on a few main applications of streaming, such as training (e-learning), corporate communications, and advertising and marketing. Although there is plenty of innovation in new applications, these categories encompass what most companies currently do with streaming. As we will show, these applications are smart choices and a good match for today's streaming technology. They bring measurable, quantifiable returns to supplement the many intangible benefits.
- Early results are very positive: Although most companies have been streaming for a relatively short period of time, they are already seeing many of the benefits they expected and desired, which include improved revenue, communication and timeliness, substantial cost savings, and customer satisfaction.
- Most companies are still at the basic webcast level: The vast majority of companies are using basic streaming technology, primarily for one-way webcasts. Few companies have begun using the more sophisticated technologies that enhance the value, and tame the complexity, of managing digital media. As the foundation of corporate streaming applications concretizes, an opportunity is presented for vendors of digital media asset management, digital rights management, and tracking and measuring solutions.
- It's growing rapidly: All key indicators—the number of companies using streaming, spending levels, the number of people served, the magnitude of stream-hours delivered, and average stream bit rates—point to significant growth and big growth potential. We're clearly in a period of rapid growth and adoption.
- Everyone is trying it: Well, almost everyone. This research includes respondents from numerous industries, such as consumer: automotive, electronics, museum, retail, and travel; financial: bank, brokerage, and services; media: advertising, cable TV, radio, recorded music, TV, video games, and webcast; technology: aviation, consulting, construction, education, events, medical, network, PC, petrochemical, pharmaceutical, recruiting, semiconductor, and software.
- The early adopters are tech savvy: The wide range of industries and company sizes represented is accompanied by one common factor: Early streaming adopters are primarily companies who are already familiar users of high technology. This is just as you would expect.

Major research conclusions

Spending

The measure of spending on products, services, staff, and supporting equipment forms the first step in calculating return on investment. An investment in technology and new ways of doing business involves more than capital outlay; it also entails a psychological commitment to change, for example. But a measurement of spending allows for apples-to-apples comparisons on overall cost savings, and serves as an indicator of commitment to and confidence in achieving less tangible returns.

These are our most important summary research conclusions on stream spending:

- The total stream spending of the 111 respondents who provided detailed spending data is $105 million. That is an average of $954,328 each. This is higher than has ever been previously reported.
- Our conservative estimate is that enterprise spending in North America will total $318 million in year 2001. Additionally, high staff and equipment costs within enterprise spending point to significant market opportunities for automation. We estimate $125 million in spending this year for companies that offer automation products and services.
- This stream spending represents just 0.12 percent (that is, one eighth of 1 percent) of the total annual revenue of these companies. Thus, we feel the capital impact is not a limiting factor, and room for growth, once benefits are realized, is substantial.

These companies served just under 3.4 million stream-hours to a total of more than 4.1 million people. (There is no doubt that there are some

Major Cost Factors

	Equipment	Staff	Network	Outsource	Production
Training	28%	35%	12%	4%	21%
Corp. Communications	19%	43%	13%	7%	19%
Advertising/Marketing	10%	47%	15%	3%	24%
Entertainment	32%	41%	11%	5%	10%

Figure B.1

duplicates between people served by different companies, but no one has a way to measure the total number of unique people served.) This means that the average person served spent just over an hour a year streaming. See Figure B.1 for a summary of total spending, stream-hours delivered, and people served as categorized by the major streaming applications used by respondents.

The importance of unit costs

The big picture represented by these data is the key to understanding streaming costs. The average cost of a stream hour, across all the above applications, is $31.35, and the average cost per person served is $25.64. These are figures that you should keep in mind as you explore this research report.

As you will see in the ROI report there are dedicated chapters on training and education and corporate communications applications (Chapters 4 and 5). In these chapters there is a wide range in spending and uses of streaming. This variation represents the research participants and, because the sample size is large enough and continuous enough, it also represents the state of the corporate streaming market.

In order to find measurement tools that are valuable across this wide range of usage, we have created two new metrics: cost per hour (CPH) and cost per person (CPP). We believe that these two metrics can be used to accurately predict the streaming costs of companies who are operating at peak efficiency. They also offer management a simple perspective on their investments in streaming.

This analogy explains the notion of unit cost at operating efficiency. The unit cost of an airline seat, the unit cost of business rental space, and the unit costs at a semiconductor fabrication plant all have this in common: A huge capital investment is made before any revenue is derived. Only when such businesses are operating at capacity will the unit costs stabilize at very flat rates. The peak efficiency costs for streaming applications have never been analyzed or published before, and yet they are very stable and predictable. This makes them extremely useful forecasting tools.

These metrics help to make some management decisions easier. It can be fairly difficult to calculate the ROI for a $500,000 project, but it's very easy to calculate the cost savings of spending $30 for an hour of employee training as compared with the alternate costs of either travel or distribution via traditional media.

The case is similar for CPP. This metric makes it easier to calculate and manage investments in terms of all other technology investments. If a company knows that its target cost for 10 hours of streamed programming will be $250 per person, it has a tool to measure against other investments, such as the cost of PC replacement or supplying soft drinks.

Major cost factors

It's also important to note just how the spending by these companies breaks down according to equipment, staff, network, outsourced services (encoding, storage, and delivery), and production (see Figure B.2). Staff costs clearly dominate spending across all streaming applications. Equipment and production constitute the second major cost center for streaming. Most spending is internal and not outsourced. And, as we will explain later, respondents may have underestimated their network costs (largely because their networks are in place and paid for, and thus appear to be "free").

Corporations (the users) should plan accordingly and understand that the primary cost center will be the staff applied to streaming initiatives. These high staff and equipment costs also represent a need for automation. So for those offering streaming and digital media products and services that address this need, they can be seen as a sign of market opportunity.

Major Cost Factors

	Equipment	Staff	Network	Outsource	Production
Training	28%	35%	12%	4%	21%
Corp. Communications	19%	43%	13%	7%	19%
Advertising/Marketing	10%	47%	15%	3%	24%
Entertainment	32%	41%	11%	5%	10%

Figure B.2

Applications Deployed

Application	Deployed
Advertising	58%
Communication	55%
Entertainment	55%
Training	51%
Conferencing	29%
Help Desk	15%
Other	5%

Figure B.3

Companies may or may not choose to outsource their streaming infra-structure. The majority of companies we interviewed manage most of their streaming infrastructure in-house. Increasing their outsourcing will primarily depend on matters of overall economics, control of network usage, system security, and quality of service.

The applications corporations deploy

Although one application is often the center focus for a company's stream-ing efforts, companies usually use streaming for more than one application. The most popular streaming applications are training, corporate communi-cations, advertising and marketing, and entertainment. Figure B.3 largely reflects the selection of companies that participated in our ROI research, and thus the percentages can't be extrapolated across all companies. Still, it's clear from our research that these are the four most common streaming applica-tions deployed today.

The two streaming applications that best represent enterprise use are training and corporate communications. This is why we devote detailed examinations to these applications (see Chapter 4: Training and Education and Chapter 5: Corporate Communications in the ROI Report). Other streaming applications are included in our summary data (and are the focus of Chapter 6: Emerging Applications).

When companies deployed streaming

It's especially important to note that the vast majority of these streaming applications were first deployed in 2000 and 2001. Just three respondents out of 111 deployed streaming applications earlier than 2000. There are certainly companies that have been streaming for a long time, but most companies are just getting started.

Market growth

The primary goal of this research and report is to identify ROI for corpo-rations employing streaming, and to establish a means of measuring it. However, because we researched the most significant measures of corporate use of streaming—spending, stream-hours delivered, how many people were served, and the duration of streams—we have been able to calculate the growth of enterprise streaming by each of these metrics.

These are our most important summary research conclusions on the market growth of streaming. By every measure, respondents' use of stream-ing is growing rapidly (compare 2001 data to 2000 data):

- 45 percent more companies are streaming this year
- 86 percent increase in total enterprise streaming spending
- 35 percent increase in the number of people served
- 230 percent increase in the total number of stream-hours delivered
- 465 percent increase in bytes transferred (suggesting that the average bit rate delivered has doubled)

Clearly, enterprise use of streaming is just now becoming mainstream. We estimate that rapid growth will continue for the next three years, as the result of these factors: (1) significantly more companies will begin trial streaming efforts; (2) companies will expand from their initial trials to reach more of their employees and customers with more content; and (3) companies will expand the range of streaming applications they employ.

Figure B.4 shows our growth predictions for enterprise streaming by application.

Why companies stream

ROI is all about expectations and actual results. ROI analysis hinges, to some degree, on why companies stream, what they consider the desired benefits of streaming, what they want to get in return, and what they actually receive in return. It may or may not be important to you exactly which benefits other companies want to achieve. But the various benefits your company wants to achieve through its streaming initiatives is very important. To reach these goals, you should concentrate on the benefits that matter most to you, and then plan how to measure them.

Part of our research reveals that corporations consider the potential benefits of streaming primarily in terms of increased revenue and communication. Quite surprisingly, increased productivity and significant cost savings

Enterprise Streaming Forecast (in Millions)

Application	Y2000	Y2001	Y2002	Y2003	Y2004
Training	$46	$87	$152	$251	$389
Corporate Communications	$48	$69	$121	$199	$309
Advertising and Marketing	$31	$77	$135	$222	$344
Entertainment	$46	$85	$127	$191	$287
Total	$171	$318	$535	$863	$1,329

Figure B.4

don't represent the primary driving force behind corporate adoption of streaming—even as these same respondents make clear exactly how much benefit they have derived in terms of productivity and cost savings. This contradiction represents the corporate focus on the bottom line, rather than a dismissal of these benefits.

Companies primarily want increased revenue and communication

- Increased revenue is desired by 74 percent of respondents—more than any other benefit.
- Improved communication is a close second at 72 percent.
- Enhanced brand follows with 68 percent.
- Despite the fact that not all of these desired benefits apply to all applications, these expectations make perfect business sense.
- What surprises us is that just 46 and 28 percent of respondents seek the potential benefits of cost savings and employee productivity, respectively.

You can't manage what you can't measure

- Whatever ROI benefits you desire, there are ways to track and manage each of them.
- Many respondents are under the illusion that streaming had already paid off, yet when we examined their cost of customer acquisition and cost of sale, they were frequently not achieving the success they imagined.
- Focus on the direct benefits (tangible and intangible) you want, rather than on the end benefits (such as revenue). This gives you something you can manage.

The perception *is* the reality

The streaming industry should take note of these perceptions in its sales and marketing collateral. Enterprise customers show little confidence in achieving increased productivity. Companies are looking for ways to see direct increases in revenue and communication from their streaming initiatives. This requires the ability to track viewing behavior directly to revenue, which is not something that any of our respondents are able to do now.

Early results

Although the vast majority of respondents have deployed streaming within just the past 18 months, they are already deriving visible benefits. Respondents have perceived an increase, if not always measurable, in the top desired benefits of revenue, communication, and brand recognition. (It should be noted that for brand recognition, the respondents were identifying a "coolness factor" or perception that implementing streaming signaled a company initiative that was unique and innovative. We expect the perceived benefit of brand recognition to diminish as streaming becomes more ubiquitous.) No respondents reported results so unsatisfactory that they were inclined to give up and stop using streaming.

Summary conclusions and predictions

Here are the main conclusions we have reached from our ROI research, along with the major predictions:

Conclusions

1. By every measure, respondents' use of streaming is growing rapidly.
   - 45 percent more companies are streaming this year.
   - There is an 86 percent increase in total enterprise spending.
   - There has been a 35 percent increase in the number of people served.
   - There is a 230 percent increase in the total of stream hours delivered.
   - There was a 465 percent increase in bytes transferred (which means that the average bit rate delivered has doubled).
2. Enterprise use of streaming is just now becoming mainstream.
3. Streaming is highly economical compared to traditional media distribution and employee travel.
   - Streaming is highly economical as compared with the cost of travel.
   - Streaming is extremely effective as compared with traditional media distribution.
   - Expansion-phase deployments experience significant economies of scale, are more efficient with resources, and deliver more benefits (to more people served, and for longer duration).
   - At peak operating efficiency, a corporation will spend approximately $20 to 31 per stream-hour, delivered (depending on the particular streaming application).

Predictions

1. Streaming usage will continue to expand rapidly in corporations worldwide.

- Enterprise stream spending in North America this year will be $318 million.
- Companies will expand from early trials into full-blown initiatives.
- Expansion-phase companies will have to manage issues of network capacity, storage systems, and more sophisticated streaming application technologies.
2. We estimate that the current 30 percent compound growth rate (CGR) will continue for the next three years, because significantly more companies will begin trial streaming efforts and companies will expand from their initial trials to reach more of their employees and customers with more content.
3. Companies will expand the range of streaming applications they employ.

Training and education

Companies put a high priority on training and continuing education for employees. W.R. Hambrecht & Company says the e-learning market will reach $11.5 billion by 2003. There are many reasons for a huge corporate investment in e-learning for training and educational purposes, most of which come down to survival in today's competitive business environment. There is an urgent need to deliver knowledge and to enhance the skills of employees and business partners right now, more effectively, and with better retention.

StreamLearning, as we will call it, is e-learning that is streamed. There are numerous reasons that companies are annually doubling their investment in StreamLearning. These include cost savings, primarily on the outright costs and lost productive time associated with employee travel; timeliness of delivery; convenience; increased reach; and retention and knowledge management.

Companies can save their knowledge in a way that can be used in multiple ways later. Companies want to compete effectively, and to do so they use StreamLearning to enhance employee performance, motivation, and innovation. The results are smarter, more effective employees accompanied by significant cost savings as compared with travel.

Why StreamLearning?

Because e-learning can be delivered by several alternative media, including audio/videotape, CD-ROM, videoconferencing, and cable and satellite broadcast, the question is: Why streaming? There are two main reasons:

1. StreamLearning is less expensive than videoconferencing (where the bandwidth costs alone are roughly five times the cost of streaming) or

satellite communications (which can cost hundreds of dollars per hour, and is generally limited to a small number of conference rooms with downlink sites).

2. StreamLearning has all of the benefits of traditional media distribution (such as videotape and CD-ROM), but with all of the additional advantages of flexibility and accessibility afforded by digital technology and Internet distribution. StreamLearning can be part of a company's public and private Web sites, allowing for interactivity, testing, tracking, and measurement of access; personalization; convenience; privacy; remote access; and repeated use.

Whether you want to train your employees, business partners, or customers to use your products or services, online multimedia education can be part of the answer. StreamLearning has many of the benefits of on-site education, but often with more attractive cost and convenience factors for both employer and employee.

StreamLearning is widely deployed in businesses and institutions of higher learning for the following applications: educational courses, product launches, product/service tutorials, case studies, and FAQ media. Wherever there is a need to inform and a subject matter that can benefit from audio/visual media, StreamLearning can be a convenient and cost-effective solution.

- Product launches: By far this is the most popular use of StreamLearning encountered in our research. Typically, this involves a live event broadcast throughout the company, followed by the ability to view (or listen) on demand. The event is usually hosted by a sales or marketing executive or a product manager. Attendees are often in remote locations, and not all are served by the corporate LAN/WAN. These events usually last no more than an hour, with two-way interaction between the presenters and the audience. The back channel for return communication from the audience is a combination of telephone, online chat, e-mail, and sometimes even satellite broadcast. On-demand viewers are able to use the one-way webcasts as well as related interactive material online.

- Educational courses: Courseware is educational material focusing on a specific topic (technology, product, marketplace). According to our research, this type of material is normally accessed on demand. Today's corporate use of such educational material is primarily via one-way webcast, accompanied by minimal related material (usually no more than hyperlinks to related research and information).

- Product/service tutorials: This kind of StreamLearning material is usually targeted at service personnel, business partners, and customers. Almost always presented as one-way video on demand, this material is available whenever the need arises. At this stage of the game, it is rarely accompanied by interactive content such as testing and compliance certification, but this is an area that holds high potential for growth.

- Case studies: Sometimes the most powerful way to communicate what a product or service does is to present successful examples of how it works. The employee, the business partner, and the customer are able to understand what is involved and what the results are by seeing for themselves.
- FAQ media: Virtually all Web sites offer information in the form of frequently asked questions (FAQs). Streaming allows this material to be provided as either audio or video, with all of the impact and explanatory power inherent in these formats.

John Chambers, Chief Executive Officer of Cisco Systems, is confident there will be a significant growth in online education. In the *New York Times* in November 2000, he said, "The next big killer application for the Internet is going to be education. Education over the Internet is going to be so big it is going to make e-mail usage look like a rounding error." Whether or not you're that confident about the importance of streamed training, our research shows that it comes down to a simple scenario: Spend around $30 for each of your employees to view streaming video (per hour of material), at their convenience and as many times as they want or need, or spend $1,000 for every person who has to travel to the city where the meeting originates. Despite the technical learning curve and equipment and staff expenses required to implement such a system, the choice is increasingly obvious to a large number of companies worldwide.

Cases in point

Below you'll find brief summaries of just a few of the ways that the companies we surveyed are using streaming in training and education applications. Expanded examples can be found later where we present ROI results. What you will see are companies that already achieve significant cost savings and other tangible benefits from their StreamLearning efforts.

Each of the case studies illuminates one of the ways that StreamLearning benefits companies who use it. Here are three examples:

1. Network equipment manufacturer reduces costs by factor of seven.
   - Spends $10 million annually on StreamLearning
   - Averages 8.5 hours streamed to each of its 42,000 employees
   - Saves at least 7 times the alternative cost of employee travel

2. Telecommunications company saves $5.5 million annually.
   - Spends $480,000 annually on StreamLearning
   - Averages 2 hours streamed to each of its 5,000 employees
   - Sales training costs dropped from $6 million/year to $500,000/year
3. Leading business school delivers more value than ever before.
   - Spends $1 million annually on StreamLearning
   - Averages 50 hours streamed to each of its 2,500 students
   - Delivers exceptional class-preparatory material that was never before available to its students

Streaming technologies are used in a variety of ways within organizations to inform and educate. At the most basic level, the user simply views a one-way webcast. The basic technology requirements, potential hurdles, and broad-based solutions are outlined in our research report in Chapter 7: Technical Requirements and Challenges.

As with any technology, in streaming the minimum is really the minimum and the quality is often unsatisfactory. However, there are products and services that can significantly address both of these issues. Moreover, a basic configuration ignores a range of more sophisticated features that can add considerably to the effectiveness and ROI of StreamLearning.

Advanced features in a corporate StreamLearning application
Interactivity

StreamLearning can include such interactive elements as slide shows, rich-media animations, and exercises. These elements engage the student more deeply in the material and offer the student hands-on practice. For example, you can add weblinks to related information and/or timely new market data and add animated demonstrations and simulations. The primary benefit of interactivity is that the audience is engaged rather than just passively viewing the material. Interactivity causes a more powerful impact, which increases memory retention of the material and makes a more effective training experience.

Although interactivity can help to make a distance learning experience more personal, StreamLearning material is most often presented in a one-way broadcast. And while interactivity can enhance a StreamLearning experience substantially, it doesn't, and perhaps can't, match the experience of classroom training. The main limiting factor in two-way, interactive streaming applications is latency in transmission, which occurs both at the streaming server and in the network. Latency may vary widely from one situation to another, but can be as little as a few seconds or as much as a few minutes. Although some latency can be tolerated for back-channel communication, at this time, it's best to use StreamLearning primarily as a one-way process, especially when both audio and video are used (the large bandwidth required for audio/video streaming increases the back-channel latency). Other means of two-way interactivity that are less limited by latency are possible in training and other applications, however, they include text-based two-way chat and shared whiteboards. These can provide immediate, direct communication between a live trainer and trainees during an audio/video streaming session without affecting streaming performance. In other words, don't try to use streaming for videoconferencing—it simply doesn't work.

Even with the benefit of interactivity, StreamLearning will simply never provide the same quality of experience as on-site education. On the other hand, StreamLearning can also exceed the richness of an on-site training experience. For example, an online syllabus might include video case studies that bring the source to the student. Moreover, the ability to access the material multiple times, whenever desired, can be a significant benefit to the user. It also enables you to test, poll, and gain feedback from your efforts.

Traditionally, you don't expect feedback, but now your data collection can give you all the information you need. The costs of adding interactivity are the same kind of costs you expect for your Web site development, and depend entirely on what you do and how much. But the returns on this investment are as significant as anything you do at your Web site.

Testing

There is no better way to evaluate what the student has learned and the educational effectiveness of the material than by testing. High technology is not necessary to do this testing. Pose a few questions that cover the messages you really want to communicate; put them in an e-mail, Word file, or spreadsheet; and have the viewers submit the completed tests. Another way to test the material's effectiveness, if you feel like tackling a relatively easy Web site improvement, is to add some interactivity such as a few questions as check boxes, multiple choices, or fill-in the blanks.

With testing, for the first time, you can measure exactly how well your training and product launch events are really working. This gives you the ability to improve the effectiveness of your material without complicated technology and in a cost-effective manner.

Polling

Polling is a means to gain audience feedback, whether it's about the streamed content itself, or the way the material is provided. Would you like to know:

1. What your sales team thinks of the new products and/or the new marketing campaign?
2. What your employees and business partners think about the new DRM technology you have just encouraged them to adopt?
3. What your customers think about your product tutorials, such as just how helpful they are?

Polling is a simple means to answer these questions. This kind of audience feedback can determine customer satisfaction and employee morale.

Tracking and measurement of access

Technology and tools are available to allow the content provider to track who is using the material, what portions they have viewed, and how often they have accessed the material. Instead of wondering what the raw stream tracking statistics mean, you can obtain real knowledge about how the material is used. Measuring access can answer all of these questions:

1. What percentage of the intended audience viewed the material?
2. What specific individuals have not yet viewed the material?
3. Who can be given an additional reminder to view the material on demand?

Personalization

This is the ability to deliver only the desired subset of the material to each audience member. Each person receives only those webcasts, or portions of webcasts, that apply to their interests. By serving people just the content that's relevant to them, you increase the effectiveness of the content they view. Because people are getting less extraneous material (i.e., no spam), they are more likely to watch what is selected specifically for them.

Database

At the highest end, StreamLearning can also involve managing a "learning experience" database by tracking test scores and tasks accomplished, along with other indicators of student progress. The database can be the center of your knowledge universe, with, among other things, the total repository of all your content, indexed content for searching and fast time-code access within clips, the record of who has viewed what, and the record of testing and polling results.

Investment

In order to evaluate the ROI of StreamLearning, we will examine how much companies are investing and what benefits they derive in return, which include cost savings, improved communication, and increased revenue. Of the 111 respondent companies, 29 said that StreamLearning is their primary use of streaming. In this section, we will examine how much corporations spend on StreamLearning.

Spending for the 29 respondent companies that reported StreamLearning as their primary streaming activity totaled $28,965,400 in 2001. This represents an 89 percent increase in spending in the year 2000 by these companies. The average spending per company is $998,807. The range of spending is $45,000 to 10,000,000, and the median spending is $280,000. It seems reasonable to use this median figure as a rough approximation of the divide between those "just testing the waters with an initial trial" (below $280,000 annual spending), and those "increasingly committed to investing in Stream-Learning." Although the average spending of $1 million is probably an inflated estimate of representative spending levels, we can use the median figure to identify those in initial trials and those in a more advanced phase of enterprise streaming.

Notably, almost two-thirds of these respondents will spend between $100,000 and 1,000,000 on streaming this year. Many of these respondents will spend more than $1 million. From virtually any angle, this indicates a robust level of spending by these companies. Beyond actual dollar spending, the best way to measure corporate investment in streaming is to count the number of people served and the number of hours streamed. These respondents will serve a total of nearly 1.2 million stream hours to 378,000 people in 2001. This means that:

- Each respondent will deliver an average of 42,584 StreamLearning hours annually. However, the median figure is just 2,400 hours annually, and only 10 percent of respondents stream 10,000 or more hours annually. Most respondents deliver between 1,000 and 8,000 stream-hours annually.
- Each respondent serves StreamLearning to an average of 13,484 people annually. The median figure is 5,000 people served annually. Most respondents serve between 1,000 and 10,000 people annually. This represents extensive reach within the corporate environment.
- Each person served averages 3.16 hours of StreamLearning annually. The median figure is roughly one hour per person, per year, which, based on our research, represents modest, trial-level use of streamed content by corporations.

In summary, both spending levels and number of people served are higher than we expected, which shows a robust adoption rate of StreamLearning. But the median measure of stream hours delivered is somewhat more modest, because many respondents only recently launched their services. Overall, respondents seem to be clearly moving from initial trials to higher investments.

The big costs
Staff and equipment

Another key research finding is the breakdown of spending among several main cost factors. These are summarized in the table in Figure B.5 (sorted by total spending). The highest cost factor for each company's total streaming spending and the second highest cost factor are both outlined in this table.

The conclusion drawn from these data is that staff and equipment costs are the biggest costs for StreamLearning. Staff costs average 35 percent of total StreamLearning spending by these companies, and equipment represents an additional 28 percent, on average. Thus, staff and equipment comprise 63 percent, or nearly two-thirds of all streaming spending by the respondent companies. A total of 41 percent of these companies reported staff costs as the top cost factor for their total stream spending.

Half of the companies whose StreamLearning costs include in-house staff spend $700,000 or more annually on staff related to streaming. This represents a sizeable, certainly non-casual, investment in staff and staff time for this application. These companies who have invested this much money have clearly moved beyond the trial stage.

For some companies equipment costs can be substantial. Most companies think of their current in-place networks as "free," either because the basic network infrastructure is already in place and paid for, or because the budget for network equipment and maintenance belongs to a department outside of the streaming initiatives, or both. When planning your streaming initiatives, be sure to avoid this fallacy. As soon as enough people within your organization begin streaming a substantial amount of high-bandwidth content, the true network costs will become all too apparent. Your costs will increase as you expand network capacity and extend services to remote connections, and you will also experience increased complexity of network and storage operations. At the same time, be sure to amortize the cost of equipment related to StreamLearning across the period it is expected to serve.

Streamed Training Spending Summary

	Equipment	Staff	Network	Outsource	Production	Total
	$4,000,000	$1,500,000	$1,500,000		$3,000,000	$10,000,000
	$1,000,000	$1,200,000		$90,000	$1,200,000	$3,490,000
	$200,000	$1,450,000	$900,000		$600,000	$3,150,000
	$625,000	$875,000		$120,000		$1,620,000
	$20,000	$1,500,000	$60,000		$10,000	$1,590,000
	$200,000	$150,000	$200,000	$100,000	$750,000	$1,400,000
	$500,000	$800,000	$80,000			$1,380,000
	$900,000	$90,000			$990,000	
	$800,000					$800,000
	$20,000	$700,000	$8,400	$8,400	$18,000	$754,800
	$300,000		$180,000	$100,000	$100,000	$680,000
		$75,000	$84,000	$175,000	$5,000	$339,000
	$320,000				$320,000	
	$62,500	$50,000	$125,000	$25,000	$37,500	$300,000
	$25,000	$50,000	$30,000	$50,000	$125,000	$280,000
	$20,000	$200,000	$20,000		$5,000	$245,000
			$28,000	$200,000		$228,000
	$20,000	$50,000		$50,000	$100,000	$220,000
	$15,000	$150,000	$20,000			$185,000
	$50,000	$75,000	$12,500	$37,500	$5,000	$180,000
	$30,000		$50,000	$30,000	$30,000	$140,000
	$5,000		$80,000		$25,000	$110,000
				$33,600	$70,000	$103,600
	$50,000				$50,000	$100,000
	$50,000	$25,000			$25,000	$100,000
	$10,000	$15,000	$30,000	$10,000	$20,000	$85,000
	$30,000	$15,000	$10,000	$15,000	$10,000	$80,000
						$50,000
	$10,000	$20,000	$10,000		$5,000	$45,000
TOTAL:	$8,042,500	$10,120,000	$3,517,900	$1,044,500	$6,190,500	$28,965,400
% OF TOTAL:	28%	35%	12%	4%	21%	100%

Yellow = Highest cost factor.
Green = Second highest cost factor.

Figure B.5

Cost per Person, Cost per Hour

	Spending	Aggregate Stream Hours	Number of Users	Hours per Person	Cost per Person	Cost per Hour
	$10,000,000	356,000	42,000	8.48	$238	$28
	$3,490,000	792,815	159,350	4.98	$22	$4
	$3,150,000	2,700	500	5.40	$6,300	$1,167
	$1,620,000	1,500	50,000	0.03	$32	$1,080
	$1,590,000		5,000		$318	
	$1,400,000	2,000	50,000	0.04	$28	$700
	$990,000	5,000	1,000	5.00	$990	$198
	$754,800		800		$944	
	$680,000		5,000		$136	
	$339,000	2,810	9,559	0.29	$35	$121
	$320,000	4,000	1,100	3.64	$291	$80
	$228,000	8,000	1,000	8.00	$228	$29
	$185,000	2,400	2,200	1.09	$84	$77
	$180,000	1,500	1,800	0.83	$100	$120
	$140,000	1,500	6,000	0.25	$23	$93
	$110,000	1,968	6,500	0.30	$17	$56
	$85,000	10,000	30,150	0.33	$3	$9
	$80,000	155	600	0.26	$133	$516
	$45,000		5,000		$9	
ENTIRE SAMPLE	$25,386,800	1,192,348	377,559	3.16	$67	$21

Figure B.6

Cost per hour, cost per person

Nineteen of these StreamLearning respondents provided detailed customer usage data. In our research, CPH for StreamLearning ranges from $4 to 1,167 (see Figure B.6). But for the majority of these companies (especially those companies whose aggregate stream hours total more than 3,000 annually), the average CPH ranges between $4 and 198.

Here's the key differentiator: The more companies spend on streaming, the more attractive their unit costs. In the sections below where we examine "trial" and "expansion" phase scenarios, it will become clear how much more economical expansion phase operations are. For now, please note that for companies that have achieved streaming usage above 8,000 aggregate stream-hours delivered annually, the unit CPH is in a relatively narrow range of $4 to 28. When operating at a high percentage of capacity, you can reasonably expect this range. The average CPH delivered is $21, and the average CPP served is $67. As you will see, these representations of unit cost are central to understanding the total value of StreamLearning.

Spending scenarios

Budgeting for your planned streamed training depends on whether or not you plan to build or buy, that is, whether you intend to outsource significant parts of the process. Alternatively, if you plan to keep these functions mostly in-house, you will have to estimate the individual costs of equipment, staff, network, and other elements that are described above.

For those who decide not to outsource, for a quick estimate of your costs, you can use the following scenarios: trial (annual spending below the median $280,000) and expansion (annual spending above $280,000).

"Trial" scenario

This scenario analyzes the expected costs for your first StreamLearning trial. In this scenario, you will very likely provide some training to a subset of all of your employees. One of the most common trial uses of StreamLearning is product launch briefings by the sales and marketing team. Using the spending patterns of those companies whose use of StreamLearning fits this trial category, the table in Figure B.7 provides a way to budget your costs. To use this

StreamLearning: "Trial" Scenario

	"Trial" Average	Range of Replies	Your "Trial" Scenario
Number of people served	6,656	600–30,150	[Step 1—How many will you serve annually?]
Annual duration per student	0.5 hours	0.3–8 hours	[Step 2—What average duration do you plan?]
Average cost per hour	$41	$9–$120	[Step 3—Use the average cost per hour: $41]
Total expected costs:	$136,448	$45,000–$228,000	[Step 4—Multiply 1, 2, & 3]

Figure B.7

table, first estimate how many people you plan to serve annually. Then estimate the average amount of material you want people to consume annually and use the average cost per stream-hour (assuming your efforts will be implemented with average efficiency). Multiply these figures, and you will have a reasonable estimate of your annual trial StreamLearning initiatives. The range of respondent data is included to show you what other companies are doing.

"Expansion" scenario

This scenario analyzes the expected costs for your StreamLearning expansion phase. In this scenario, you will expand your initiative to a much larger subset of all of your employees, which results in lower costs overall. Using the spending patterns of those companies whose use of StreamLearning fits this expansion category, the table in Figure B.8 provides a way to budget your costs.

Unit costs

As the above sections illustrate, the basic economics of the trial and expansion phases are quite different. Trial phase companies serve fewer people, less time per person (half an hour, on average), and incur a higher cost per hour ($41 average). Expansion phase companies serve more hours (3.6 hours average) to more people, at a lower cost per hour ($21 average).

Expansion brings economies of scale and is more efficient with resources, at the same time it delivers more benefits (more people served and longer).

StreamLearning "Expansion" Scenario

	"Trial" Average	Range of Replies	Your "Trial" Scenario
Number of people served	29,483	500–159,350	[Step 1—How many will you serve annually?]
Annual duration per student	3.6 hours	0.3–8.5 hours	[Step 2—What average duration do you plan?]
Average cost per hour	$21	$9–$120	[Step 3—Use the average cost per hour: $41]
Total expected costs:	$2,228,914	$320,000–$10,000,000	[Step 4—Multiply 1, 2, & 3]

Figure B.8

The smart approach is first to launch a trial application (annual cost below $300,000) to determine the benefits, problems, solutions, and overall results. The next step is to expand throughout the enterprise based on need and potential benefits (such as cost savings).

ROI

Even though the vast majority of these StreamLearning services were only recently launched (in 2000 to 2001), the respondents are already starting to achieve some degree of their anticipated benefits. Of the respondents, 40 to 50 percent report improved communication, revenue, branding, audience retention, and cost savings (all of the benefits they most desired). However, it must be strongly emphasized that most respondents do not actually measure their streaming ROI or communication, brand, cost savings, revenue, impact, and audience retention. What they reported are their impressions and feelings about their results.

These data are an accurate reflection of the fact that many respondents are confident they have already achieved at least some of their primary expected benefits. These data simply mean that these companies are happy with their early results and expect even better results in the future. In the following section, we use CPH and CPP unit costs derived from our research data to calculate real cost savings scenarios and show cost savings potential for your business.

Cost savings
Analysis

In this section, we put our CPH and CPP metrics to work to help determine total potential cost savings ROI for your business. Your cost savings, and thus a good part of your ROI, may vary significantly from the data presented in this chapter, but it will depend primarily on these three variables: the cost of streaming, the cost of travel for your employees, and the cost of unproductive employee down time.

1. The cost of streaming will be determined by:
   - Whether or not your streaming is confined to the internal network or operates across the open Internet (bandwidth costs)
   - Whether you are streaming audio or video, and the mix of streaming bit rates you support (audio only is far more economical than video to stream)
   - Whether or not you outsource any of the operations
2. The cost of travel for your employees depends on what percentage of trainees would need to travel to each event, and where they are going.

Cost Savings Calculator

Cost per Hour	Cost per Person	Travel Cost	Cost Savings	ROI%
$10	$30	$500	$450	1,500%
$50	$150	$500	$350	233%
$100	$300	$500	$200	67%

Figure B.9

3. The cost of unproductive employee down time is easily calculated in most companies. It's the range of hourly or daily costs of employees.

To calculate potential cost savings, see the table in Figure B.9. If you can achieve an efficient cost of streaming, and assuming an average per-person travel cost of $500, then the ROI (cost savings divided by the cost) is a factor that ranges from 10 to 50 times costs. This does not even include the value of unproductive employee time while traveling.

Your average travel costs may be quite different from $500 per person. To determine your potential cost savings, you should substitute your expected average per-person travel costs. First, determine how many people would otherwise need to travel. Then estimate their average travel costs (based on standard travel costs for your business). Next, estimate your possible streaming costs by multiplying your expected hourly cost (try several cost levels, from $10 to 100 per hour), by the number of StreamLearning hours planned per person (the above scenarios assume three hours per person, per year). The ROI estimate is calculated by dividing the cost savings by the streaming costs.

Real world examples

Below are five detailed examples, culled from our research, of companies that have already achieved significant cost savings through their StreamLearning initiatives.

Network equipment manufacturer reduces costs by factor of seven

A leading network equipment manufacturer spends $10 million annually to provide new product training via video StreamLearning to its 42,000 worldwide employees and business partners. Employees receive an average of 8.5 hours of StreamLearning annually. The company delivers an annual total of 356,000 StreamLearning hours and serves 90,000 streams per month, with an average duration per session of 20 minutes. This translates to an average cost of $28/stream-hour, or annual spending of $238 per person served. This is an example of a highly economical use of StreamLearning.

"Streaming decreases employee time to competency, versus killing time to market," said a company principal. This company outsources 90 percent of its audio and video production, which costs $1,200 per finished stream-ready hour. It calculates its StreamLearning ROI against travel costs and expenses. Without streaming, one-third of all employees would have to travel in order to view this material. These costs would exceed seven times the total cost of streaming, not including the cost of employee down time. Alternatively, the total cost of creating, managing, and shipping videotapes to all employees would exceed the cost of streaming.

Semiconductor maker saves more than $400,000 a year

A leading semiconductor maker spends $100,000 annually to provide video content to 500 of its 42,000 employees. The company delivers an annual total of 2,500 StreamLearning hours. This equates to an average cost of $40 per stream-hour, and annual spending of $200 per person served. Although these costs are higher than the respondent average costs, this still reflects significant cost savings for the company, because streaming replaces annual costs of $500,000 in live on-site training. As an added benefit, this makes the training more convenient for employees.

Without streaming, 100 percent of these new sales employees would have to travel in order to participate in this class. Total company-wide travel costs would exceed 3.5 times the total cost of streaming (not including the cost of employee down time). Shipping videotapes to these employees is not a workable alternative, as the company feels it would not provide adequate training. This application constitutes a successful trial deployment of StreamLearning for the chipmaker.

College saves money for students

One of the largest universities in the United States spends $60,000 annually to provide video content (primarily course work) to the 300 of its 30,000 students who attend courses off campus via broadband connections. Averaging 12.5 hours per year per student, this represents a total of 3,750 StreamLearning hours delivered. This equates to an average cost of $16 per stream-hour, which is below the average cost of all StreamLearning respondents. The annual cost per person served is $200.

Without streaming, 100 percent of these students would have to travel in order to participate in this class. Total student travel costs would exceed five times the total cost of streaming (not including unproductive time). As in the previous case study, the school felt that videotapes just wouldn't provide the viable training necessary for these students. Again, this constitutes a very successful trial deployment of StreamLearning.

Telecom network saves $5.5 million

A leading telecommunications network spends $480,000 annually to provide video content (primarily new product training) to its 5,000 employees. Averaging two hours annually per employee, this totals 10,000 Stream-Learning hours delivered. This equates to an average cost of $48 per stream-hour, or annual spending of $96 per person served. By providing monthly sales force training via streaming instead of on-site conferences, the company realizes a significant cost savings: Sales training costs dropped from $6 million per year to $500,000 per year, not including the cost of employee down time.

Without streaming, almost half of this company's worldwide employees would have to travel in order to view this material. Total company-wide travel costs would exceed 2.5 times the total cost of streaming (not including unproductive employee time). The alternative total cost of creating, managing, and shipping videotapes to all employees would exceed the cost of streaming.

Consulting company saves money for its clients

A new media consulting and production company has several clients who have already seen the benefits of StreamLearning. A medical services client spent $35,000 to stream a live all-day event to 500 people worldwide, rather than bearing the expected $500,000 cost of hosting the event on-site (based on past events costs). Another client, a top financial services firm, spends roughly $200,000 annually to provide daily video to each of its 1,000 employees located worldwide. The cost is lower than all alternatives, including shipping videotapes, and is far more timely.

Productivity

Below are detailed examples of two organizations that have already achieved significant productivity through their StreamLearning initiatives. Sales executives love StreamLearning because it saves them considerable travel time. CFOs love it because it's an easy way to significantly reduce training costs (employees, business partners, customers). Employees like it because it's much more convenient to view a video online than to travel somewhere (even at the same location) to participate, and it's also more private.

Top 10 storage appliance maker: keeping sales people happy

One of the top 10 storage appliance makers spends $225,000 annually to provide video content (primarily for new product training) to the 300 sales people among its 2,000 employees. Averaging 12 hours annually per employee, this totals 3,600 StreamLearning hours delivered. This equates to an average cost of about $63 per stream-hour, or annual spending of $750 per person served. Rather than flying the 500-person sales team to California (or transporting director-level sales managers around the world for a 30-day sales junket), the company broadcasts new product briefings via streaming. Although the company appreciates the cost savings, it is the benefit of timely delivery of the new product information, and the reduced travel wastage of the sales team that this company appreciates most.

Business school: doing things they couldn't do before

A prestigious business school spends $1 million annually to provide video content (primarily business case studies) to all of its 2,500 students. They average 50 hours of case study StreamLearning annually per student. Including all uses of streaming, their use of StreamLearning content totals 300,000 hours delivered annually. This equates to an average cost of just over $3 per stream-hour, an annual spending of $400 per person served. A stream-hour cost of $3 is extremely economical, and among the least expensive video costs we have encountered. This low cost occurs because this university has no network or staff costs involved as they are already in place for other university use.

According to the school, providing videotapes to these students is not a workable alternative, as this would not provide adequate or timely training. Because of streaming they have enhanced the basic video material with Web site interactivity, including links to reference material, exercises, and online discussions. These would not be included in a videotape presentation. This university considers streaming essential because of the "competitive cost of not doing it." The total package of exclusive preparatory material, combined with interactivity and online student/teacher discussions, is not something that was possible before they began streaming.

Revenue

Although increased revenue is usually not a direct result of corporate StreamLearning, here is a detailed example of an organization that has achieved a revenue increase through its StreamLearning initiatives.

American Gem Trade Association helps its members, and their customers, and their customers

The American Gem Trade Association (AGTA) recently launched a massive new initiative to greatly increase the sales of colored gemstones. At the heart of this marketing campaign is a streamed training video that helps every element of the gemstone food chain: the end customers who buy the stones, jewelry stores, the association members, and the association itself. This is how it works.

The AGTA's campaign centers on a new certification that will guarantee a "Consumer Seal of Confidence." The association logo can only be used by certified members who adhere to a strict code of behavior that includes disclosure and ethics. Jewelry stores will want to have the logo on their doors, customers will want to buy gemstones that are sold by certified jewelers, members will use this certification to increase sales, and the association will achieve consistent ethical standards among its membership and retailers.

The industry has never done anything like this before, because the costs of traditional media delivery are simply not cost-effective. Gemstone training videos cost roughly $1,000, and that is considered too much to invest in the high-turnover staff common in jewelry stores. Now, the attractive economics of streaming make it possible to help everyone involved in the sale and purchase of gemstones. AGTA sells its training material to its members (roughly at cost) and to jewelry stores (at a higher sales price), which generates revenue for the association. The AGTA members, meanwhile, learn to sell colored gemstones, thus increasing their gemstone sales. This gives AGTA something additional to offer to jewelers who buy large consignments: The training video becomes a valuable give-away to help make the sale. End consumers who want to be more educated about what is involved, what must be disclosed, and whom to trust (jewelers with the logo, of course), will find the free consumer streaming videos valuable.

Timeliness

Below is a detailed example of an organization that has achieved very positive results from timely education through its StreamLearning initiatives.

Fire department trains without leaving the station

The Tulsa Fire Department (TFD) in Oklahoma uses StreamLearning. For the first time, cadets and veteran firefighters in 33 worksites serving 400,000 Tulsa residents will receive 60 percent of all their training while at their posts via streaming video. The distance training includes Emergency Medical Services and other emergency response training. With quick response times for emergencies critical to maintaining excellent service, the TFD deployment represents a significant gain for both distance learning applications and the community the department serves.

StreamLearning summary

Conclusions

These are the main conclusions reached from our StreamLearning research:

1. StreamLearning is extremely economical as compared with the cost of travel.
2. Cost per hour is $21 at peak operating efficiency.
3. StreamLearning is extremely effective in achieving reach as compared with traditional media distribution.
4. Expansion phase deployments:
   - Experience significant economies of scale
   - Are more efficient with resources
   - Deliver more benefits (to more people served, and for longer duration)

Predictions

1. StreamLearning usage will continue to expand rapidly in corporations worldwide.
2. For the next three years there will be a 35 percent annual compound growth rate in companies who are StreamLearning.
3. Average annual spending will double by 2003, as companies move from trials to expansion.
4. Companies currently in trial phase will expand to full-blown initiatives.
5. Expansion phase companies will have to manage issues of network capacity, storage systems, and more sophisticated streaming application technologies.

Glossary

add-on   Software that is designed to enhance or expand the capabilities of other software. For example, iQfx would be considered an add-on to RealPlayer because it enhances audio quality.

ADSL   (asymmetric digital subscriber line) Technology to carry high-speed data over ordinary phone lines. It is up to 70 times as fast as a 28.8 modem, and can be used concurrently with voice over the same line. It is called asymmetric because download speeds to the subscriber are faster than upload speeds from the subscriber.

algorithm   A complex mathematical procedure or formula that seeks out repetitive data and replaces it with a code. More advanced algorithms take into consideration the limitations of human perception. An algorithm determines how to compress and decompress data.

analog   Analog technology refers to electronic transmission accomplished by adding signals of varying frequency or amplitude to carrier waves of a given frequency of alternating electromagnetic current. Broadcast and phone transmission have conventionally used analog technology. Standard audiotape and videotape recordings are produced by an analog process, as a continuous wave, rather than digitally in a binary form.

applet   An application that is downloaded from a Web page and executed by browser software. Also, an HTML tag defines an applet program.

application   Software designed for a particular purpose (i.e., word processing, creating streaming content, or browsing the Internet).

archive   Information or content that has been stored in a
                               retrievable format. For example, a music video
                               selected from the Real Guide.

ASF   (advanced streaming format) An audio or video
                               file encoded for use with Windows Media Player.

ASP   A scripting environment for the Microsoft Internet
                               information server in which you can combine
                               HTML, scripts, and reusable ActiveX server com-
                               ponents to create dynamic Web pages.

aspect ratio   The relationship of the height and width of a video
                               on a monitor, for example, letterbox format is 16:9.

authentication   Request for permission from a server or user,
                               usually based on parameters set by the software
                               owner. Various types of authentication are used in
                               the Helix Universal Server.

AVI   (audio video interleaved) A Microsoft video
                               format containing multiple streams of different
                               types of data, such as audio and video. AVI files will
                               end with a .avi extension.

backbone   A central network connecting other networks
                               together.

bandwidth   The amount of data, typically expressed as kilobits
                               per second (Kbps), that can pass through a
                               network connection.

bit   Short for "binary digit," a bit has either a value of
                               one or zero and is the smallest unit of measure of
                               data in a computer.

bit rate   A measure of bandwidth, expressed as the num-
                               ber of bits transmitted per second. A 28.8-Kbps
                               modem, for example, can transmit or receive
                               around 29,000 bits per second.

broadband   Used to describe a network connection that sup-
                               ports a relatively high bit rate. Also used to
                               describe content that takes advantage of a high bit
                               rate connection.

broadcast   To deliver a presentation, whether live or prere-
                               corded, in which all viewers join the presentation
                               in progress.

browser   The program that finds and displays Web pages.
                               Microsoft Internet Explorer and Netscape Naviga-
                               tor are browsers.

buffering	Similar to caching, buffering is the process by which streaming media enters a user's computer at a faster rate than can be played. It is saved as memory without backing up or overloading the player.
byte	Short for "binary term," a byte is a unit of memory made of eight bits. It is the amount needed by a computer to store a typed number or letter.
cache	(pronounced *cash*) This is the computer memory that stores information most frequently used. Usually stored in a special section of the main memory or in a separate device, these data can be retrieved much faster than if the computer has to find it on the hard drive.
capture	Process of digitizing audio and video content from an analog format.
CDN	(content delivery network) Infrastructure providers with distributed server architectures who provide value to broadcasting customers through guaranteed delivery qualities and/or value-added services.
client	A software application that receives data from a server. A Web browser is a client of a Web server, for example, RealPlayer is typically a client of RealSystem Server.
codec	Coder/decoder. Codecs convert data between uncompressed and compressed formats, which reduces the bandwidth a clip consumes.
compression	By compressing data, your computer uses less memory to store information. When data is compressed and sent over the Web, it takes up less bandwidth and allows faster and more efficient downloading.
data	Information in the form of words, numbers, or images that has been transcribed into bits. This information can then be read by a computer and stored as memory or sent over the Internet.
data type	(media type) File format that travels across the RealSystem architecture to RealPlayers.

decode   In multimedia, this term refers to decompressing a compressed (encoded) file so that it may be displayed. Codecs do this decoding while the video/audio is played.

digital media   Sound, pictures, text, and video available in digital format for downloading or streaming across the Internet or other network.

digitizing   Process of capturing or "bringing in" audio and/or video (usually analog source tapes such as Beta SP, 3/4, VHS, etc.) into a computer. Digitizing is made possible by video hardware, a computer hardware card, cables, and a software application that all work together to convert the original signal into digital media. This digital media can then be edited and transferred back to numerous formats for Internet streaming, CD-Rom, DVD, and other forms of distribution.

download   NOUN: The software that is literally loaded or installed onto your computer from the Web, as opposed to installation via CD-ROM or other physical storage device. VERB: To receive software over the Internet.

DRM   (digital rights management) A set of technology and rules that allows content owners to set rights on how, when, and with what frequency end users can view content.

DSL   (digital subscriber lines) High speed Internet access lines for connections directly from a telephone switching station to a home or office that avoid the slowdown between switching stations. DSL offers download rates many times faster than a 56-k modem.

embedded player   A RealPlayer placed within a browser window so that only the media clip shows.

encoder   A hardware or software application used to compress audio and video signals for the purposes of streaming.

encoding   The act of rewriting or transferring media sources from one format to another (i.e., from VHS tape to RealVideo).

end user   It is IT speak for the audience or person who sat at their computer surfing the Internet and watching a webcast.

enterprise   A corporate organization. As a customer group, the term enterprise refers to customers who own and deploy across an intranet. In the streaming media industry, most vendors reference enterprise as a company in the Fortune 1000.

firewall   The concept of a security interface or gateway between a closed system or network and the outside Internet that blocks or manages communications in and out of the system. The security may be provided by passwords, authentication techniques, software, and hardware.

Flash   Refers to Web animation software created by Macromedia Inc., which has become an industry standard for Web page development.

format   Different programs and devices store information in a variety of ways. The specific arrangements of information a program or device requires is called its format. Some types of formatting are VHS, DVD, RealAudio, etc.

FTP   (file transfer protocol) The Internet protocol that permits you to transfer files between your system and another system.

GIF   (graphics interchange format) A graphics format in which images are constructed of tiny dots, also called pixels. Each one is colored to correspond to the specific area of the image they represent. This format can be compressed to require fewer memory resources, which is useful when adding images to Web pages.

graphics   Everything on a Web page that is not text based— pictures, borders, and illustrations—is graphics. Anything that is produced using a graphics program, even a text title, is considered a graphical element, because it is formatted differently than the plain text that follows it.

GSM	(global system for mobile communications) GSM is a digital wireless technology standardized to create a compatible wireless network across Europe. GSM is still most commonly used in Europe, but it is also deployed in other areas of the world. It operates in three frequency ranges: GSM 900, GSM 1800, and GSM 1900 (also called PCS 1900).
hosting	Storing media files on servers specifically designed for streaming over the Internet.
HTML	(hypertext markup language) The simple, tag-based language used to create World Wide Web pages.
hyperlink	A link in a Web page that brings you to another location or resource when activated. Hyperlinks usually appear as underlined text and are printed in a contrasting color, but they may also appear as graphics, such as buttons to click. Hyperlinks may link to another place in the same page, to a different page, to play an audio or video file, to download a file, to set up a message to an e-mail address, to search a database, to read Usenet newsgroups, and to link to other Internet resources.
image	The visual representation of illustrations, photos, and anything graphic in nature.
Internet	A network of many networks that interconnect worldwide and use the Internet Protocol (IP).
Internet broadcasting	Capturing, encoding, and hosting a live event, such as a concert, award show, meeting, or conference, usually from a remote location, for Internet broadcast on a one-time or limited basis. Live events usually require establishing an Internet connection and/or satellite uplinks for streaming over the Internet. Live events can also be archived for viewing on demand.
intranet	The internal communications network used by corporations and businesses for data sharing, presentations, or other business applications.
IP	The network layer for the TCP/IP protocol suite widely used on Ethernet networks, defined in STD 5, RFC 791. IP is a connectionless, best effort

packet-switching protocol. It provides packet routing, fragmentation, and reassembly through the data link layer.

IP address   IPs, together with domain address, are the two forms of Internet addresses mostly commonly used. IP addresses consist of four numbers between 0 and 255 separated by dots.

ISDN   (integrated services digital network) A technology that carries data over phone lines at up to 128 Kbps for dial-up users, but extends to fast broadband communications, too. It applies to the first three layers of the OSI and TCP/IP models.

ISP   (Internet service provider) A company that provides personal or business access to the Internet. Many ISPs have a RealNetworks server available to stream media clips.

Java   A programming language developed by Sun Microsystems based on C++. It is used to create Web pages that run on different platforms.

javascript   A script language (with little in common with Java) developed by Netscape for writing short programs embedded in a Web page. It is supported by Microsoft and AOL browsers starting with version 4.0.

JPEG   (joint photographic experts group) A compression technique for photos that reduces them to a small percentage of the original file size.

Kbps   (kilobits per second) The rate at which data are sent over a communication line. The typical household modem runs at 56.6 Kpbs.

LAN   Local area network.

language   Like human languages, programming languages involve sets of rules and syntax that computers understand. This allows computers to carry out the tasks set by the program. Language can refer to many different types and levels of programming languages, each with particular capabilities and shortfalls.

live signal acquisition   Acquisition of a broadcast signal from a satellite, Vyvx, microwave, or fiber optic. Live signal acquisition allows traditional media producers a cost-effective way to simulcast original broadcast content over the Internet.

media   This is the blanket term used when referring to audio, video, or images such as photos, as well as the ways they are used to reach the viewer (i.e., streaming media).

memory   The actual amount of data a computer can store either on a disk or on a chip. Disk memory is a more archival form of storage because it can be saved even when the computer is off. Chip memory is more immediately accessible, but requires electric current to actively remember information.

metadata   Additional, related information that can be stored as part of the compressed file or kept in a separate database. Examples include CD cover art, movie one-sheet images, or text-based information, such as author, title, etc.

metafile   A graphics format that combines the features of bitmap and vector graphics. Common types of metafile formats are CGM, Corel Draw CDR files, encapsulated Postscript EPS files, Adobe Illustrator, Word Perfect Graphics WPG files, PICT, and RTF.

modem   (modulator/demodulator) A modem is used between a computer and a phone or cable line to convert the computer's digital signal to an analog signal for the line and vice versa.

MP3   (MPEG, audio layer 3) A format used for the compression and reproduction of CD-quality audio, which can be downloaded and listened to on a computer or handheld device.

MPEG   A set of digital video compression standards and file formats developed by the Moving Picture Experts Group. There are three major MPEG standards: MPEG-1, MPEG-2, and MPEG-4.

multicast   A process that allows a server to send one stream to multiple recipients. This is different from traditional streaming media, where each user connects separately to a server.

network
A group of computers linked together, usually by phone lines that can share information and resources. When you are connected to the Internet, your computer is part of a network.

narrowband
Used to describe a connection over a computer network that supports a relatively low bit rate. Also sometimes used to describe content optimized for such connections.

narrowcast
Used to send data to a specific list of recipients. On the Internet, narrowcasting also refers to programming developed for "niche" interest groups.

net congestion
Traffic on the network that slows the transmission of data.

on-demand
Archived or stored content that viewers can access whenever they want, as opposed to live or one-time-only broadcast events.

packet
A small part of a message (i.e., e-mail or streaming media clip) that contains data and a destination address which is sent over a network. Parceling messages into smaller pieces and sending them one packet at a time puts a far lighter load on network resources than sending an entire file all at once.

packet loss
Data is transmitted in small units known as packets. Occasionally, packets are lost or delayed due to network congestion, which results in dropped frames.

PDF
(portable document format) Developed by Adobe Systems, PDF documents are usually used to present longer or more technical information because they open in a window outside of the page from which they are linked. This saves space on Web pages while keeping the information handy.

pixel
One unit of screen information. A video image is composed of individual colored dots referred to as pixels. Depending on how a monitor is set, a pixel can take up 8 bits/1 byte (256 colors), 16 bits/2 bytes (high color), or 24 bits/3 bytes (true color).

platform
Often used to define the operating system your computer runs on (i.e., Windows, Macintosh,

Linux), but can also refer to your computer hardware (i.e., Macintosh or PC).

player window   The window in your media player that allows you to watch streaming media content.

plug in   A type of software that adds a specific capability to a program already on your computer. For instance, your browser probably requires a plug in to see certain types of animation.

pointer files   Text files that point to the actual location (server and file name) of a streaming file. Almost all systems use pointer files.

port   A connection to a computer to enable other devices, such as printers, modems, monitors, keyboards, mice, etc., to interface with the computer. It is a logical connection to a network.

PowerPoint   Microsoft Office software that lets you create slide- and narration-enhanced business presentations.

presentation   Refers to a slide- and/or narration-based business meeting aid.

progressive download   A method of delivering audio/video data over the Internet that involves playing the downloaded portion of a file while the download is still in progress; also referred to as "pseudo-streaming."

protocol   An agreed upon format for transmitting data between two devices. The protocol determines the type of error checking to be used, the data compression method, and the method for discussion between the sending and receiving device. From a user's point of view, the only interesting aspect about protocols is that your computer or device must support the right ones if you want to communicate with other computers (see webopedia.com).

proxy   A server that sits between a client (in our case the RealOne Player) and a server. The proxy intercepts requests to see if it can fulfill the requests itself. If not, it forwards the request to the real server. In the digital media world, proxies are used to improve end-user experience and reduce bandwidth.

QuickTime   Multimedia architecture developed by Apple and used by software tool vendors and content creators to store, edit, and play synchronized graphics, sound, video, and music.

ram   A metafile which points to a RealMedia file.

real time   The actual time an event takes place. For example, real time can refer to a live broadcast or an active exchange between a host and user.

RealAudio   The file format developed by RealNetworks that is used to stream audio over the Internet.

RealMedia   Brand name describing file formats, server software, player software, and protocols used by streaming media systems from RealNetworks, which is a leading streaming media platform vendor.

RealOne Player   RealNetworks software that lets you play multimedia presentations streamed by a RealNetworks server or a Web server.

RealPix   A RealNetworks format (file extension .rp) for streaming still images over a network.

RealText   A RealNetworks format (file extension .rt) for streaming text over a network. It uses a markup language for formatting text.

RealVideo   The file format developed by RealNetworks that is used to stream video over the Internet.

resolution   Described in dots per inch (dpi), resolution refers to the clarity and detail of an image. On a 15-inch monitor there are usually 680 pixels of width, times 480 lines of height. This multiplies to a total of around 300,000 pixels, or a resolution of around 50 dpi. The higher the dpi, the more clear and precise the image will appear.

resources   The term used to describe anything you draw upon and need for a particular task. For example, e-mailing a large file requires network resources, which include the size of the server, the speed of connection, scalability, etc.

rich media   Media that has been enhanced with animation or video. Rich-media ads are animated, and often streamed, so that they appear more like television commercials as opposed to ads containing static images and text. They can be embedded in Web pages and inserted into or between video clips. Using SMIL, they can be streamed concurrent to audio programming.

RTP   (real-time transport protocol) An end-to-end network transport protocol suitable for applications transmitting real-time data (such as audio, video, or simulation data) over multicast or unicast network services.

RTSP   (real-time streaming protocol) An application-level protocol used to control the delivery of data with real-time properties. RTSP provides an extensible framework to enable controlled, on-demand delivery of real-time data, such as audio and video. Sources of data can include both live data feeds and stored clips.

SDK   (software development kit) An SDK is a group of products and/or software that helps a programmer develop applications for a specific platform.

server   A software application, such as a Web server or Helix Universal Server, that sends clips over a network. It is also a computer that runs server software.

signal   When you send an e-mail, for example, it is delivered via a signal—a bundle of information containing your message that travels over the phone lines. A television signal, on the other hand, is data that are transmitted over the airwaves which tell your television what colors to show and what sounds to produce.

simulated live   Describes a completed audio/video program which is presented on the Web as though it were live. Audience members must *tune in* to the program. If the scheduled start time has already passed, audience members will join the program in progress.

SMIL   (synchronized multimedia integration language) This is a markup (layout) language based on XML that allows content owners to divide the

RealPlayer area into static images, text, video, and slides similar to laying out a Web page.

storage device Storage device refers to many kinds of hardware used to save data. These all come with memory, which is available on either a portable disk, a hard drive disk, or digital tape.

stream To send a media clip over a network so that it begins playing back as quickly as possible.

streaming media An Internet data transfer technique that allows the user to see and hear audio and video files without lengthy download times. The host or source "streams" small packets of information over the Internet to the user, who can then access the content as it is received.

SureStream A technology that allows switching between higher and lower bandwidth streams in a single RealAudio or RealVideo file to compensate for network congestion. Available in RealSystem G2 and later versions.

T-1 A digital communications circuit that transmits at 1.54 Mbps (equals approximately 53 28.8-k modems).

T-3 A digital communications circuit that transmits at 45 Mbps (equals approximately 1,548 28.8-k modems).

tag A programming language tool that contains formatting directions.

transcoding The conversion of one digital file format to another digital file format (i.e., MP3 to Windows Media). The ideal method for encoding to multiple streaming media formats is to use the original, uncompressed source material and encode it into the new formats, which avoids transcoding completely.

transmit/transmission Used in the context of television-style broadcasting, as well as in reference to digital communication over phone or cable lines between computers.

unicast A process which forces each individual user to make an individual connection to a server to receive a stream.

upload	To transfer a file from your computer system to another system via a modem over telephone or cable lines or a telco connection using a transfer protocol. It is also a transfer from your system to a remote system.
URL	(universal resource locator) A location description that lets a Web browser or RealOne Player receive a clip stored on a Web server or RealNetworks server.
VBR	(variable bit rate) This refers to the ability to maintain a quality broadcast without interruption from fluctuating bandwidth or other network load problems.
vector graphics	Refers to graphics based on mathematical algorithms. As opposed to GIF or PNG pixel-based graphics, vector graphics can be resized infinitely without losing clarity.
VOD	(video-on-demand) Describes video content which may be viewed by the end user from beginning to end, at any time.
VOIP	(voice over IP) The practice of using an Internet connection to pass voice data using an IP instead of the standard public switched telephone network. This allows a remote worker, for instance, to function as if directly connected to a PBX even while at home or in a remote office. In bypassing the public network, it also avoids standard long distance charges, as the only connection is through an ISP. VOIP is used to keep corporate telephone costs down.
W3C	(World Wide Web Consortium) This is an Internet standards body.
WAN	Wide area network.
wav	A sound format developed by Microsoft and used extensively in Microsoft Windows.
webcast	The broadcasting of streaming content over the Internet. Typically refers to a live broadcast.
webcasting	A live broadcast format over the World Wide Web.
Windows Media	The streaming media platform released by Microsoft.

Windows Media Audio (WMA) Describes an audio file format associated with the Windows Media platform.

WMV (Windows media video) Windows Media Player 7.

Index